Berlitz®

Naples, Capri
& the Amalfi Coast

Front cover: Sorrento, Bay of Naples

Right: Dancing faun statue, Pompeii

Pompeii's Villas •
Casa del Fauno is a classic example of the town's wonderfully preserved Roman residences *(page 54)*

The Blue Grotto •
Capri's most celebrated attraction has been on the tourist itinerary for nearly 200 years *(page 69)*

Naples' Archaeological Museum • An unrivalled collection of ancient sculpture, mosaics and paintings *(page 36)*

The Museo Nazionale di Capodimonte • One of Italy's finest picture galleries *(page 39)*

Villa Cimbrone in Ravello This clifftop town captivated Wagner, D.H. Lawrence, Greta Garbo and many others *(page 85)*

Naples' Duomo At the heart of the ancient centro storico *(page 33)*

Naples, birthplace of the pizza Still the best place on earth to sample the genuine article *(page 98)*

Herculaneum Its ruins have yielded even more treasures than Pompeii *(page 59)*

Positano One of the most beautiful villages on the Amalfi coast *(page 81)*

Piazza del Plebiscito This vast semicircular square is home to the massive church of San Francesco di Paola *(page 23)*

CONTENTS

65

78
74

Features

INTRODUCTION

Naples is a theatre. Its buildings are arranged on hillsides like box seats encircling a stage. And what a set! Viewed from the heights, a castle seems to plunge like a ship into the waves of a blue sea; there's a sail or two on the water; the coastline curls past the purple cone of Vesuvius towards Sorrento's cape, and Capri floats in a distant haze. Add a little mandolin music and the curtain goes up on Act I. The good news is, the curtain never comes down.

On the corner, a wizened *signora* crochets beside a tray of contraband cigarettes she's selling, ignored by two policemen. They are arguing about Sunday's football match. From a doorway, where two men are playing cards, an appetising smell of cooking drifts into the street. Near a church, someone consults a guidebook – that's you, the tourist, a part of the action, too.

For all its social problems, Naples is a city of incredible beauty and vitality. The noise, chaos and dilapidated areas are impossible to ignore but for each crumbling tenement block there's a magnificent baroque church or ancient monument. The food, particularly the pizza, is unforgettable. But the main attraction is the street theatre laid on by the exuberant Neapolitans. Nothing beats just losing yourself in the crowded ancient streets and absorbing all the sights, smells and sounds. And when you've reached sensory overload,

Neapolitan laundry

Divided opinion

Writer Peter Nichols once declared: 'Neapolitans still reproduce what must be the nearest equivalent to life in classical times. Naples is one of the great tests. Some people hate it and some people love it.' He added: 'I think that people who do not like Naples are afraid of something.'

you can escape to the islands and coastal resorts, which are never more than an hour away.

From dramatic Naples it is just a short ferry ride to Capri, Ischia and the Amalfi coast. Nowadays most holidaymakers hurry straight to the docks and glimpse the city only in transit to these siren lands, or on a day's excursion to Pompeii and Vesuvius. A new generation of travellers has forgotten that Naples is one of Europe's oldest and greatest cities, the capital of an ancient kingdom and the one-time goal of all would-be sophisticates making the Continental 'Grand Tour'.

The vitality behind the poverty, and the beauty amid squalor, have always been part and parcel of the contradictions of Naples. It may come as a surprise to find that its treasures are all still here, and that Naples is experiencing a new popularity among Italians and foreigners alike as a vibrant and unique cultural destination that once set it apart.

Santa Lucia: once a fishing port, now a popular place to dine

Colourful Campania

Campania, the region Naples rules, is justly praised as spectacularly beautiful. It used to be the Riviera of the anicent Romans, devoted to a hedonistic pleasure and luxury still beckoning in the ruins of Pompeii and Herculaneum, and never more seductive than today in the *dolce far niente* of jet-set 'fishing villages' and flowery café terraces high above the sparkling azure sea. The Ravello that captivated Wagner in the 19th century wooed Garbo with the same allure in the 20th. The Sorrento that Caruso loved still echoes his serenade. And the Positano that Steinbeck found a dream is every bit as charming today.

Campania is also famous as the birthplace of that culinary icon, the pizza; as the unchallenged champion of pasta, with sauces based on plump tomatoes grown in rich volcanic soil; and as the home of irresistible ice creams and pastries. The fires that smoulder beneath Vesuvius heat the waters and radioactive mud of Campania's spas, renowned for their healing properties for more than 2,000 years. So if you overindulge in the wonderful food of the region, a cure is at hand.

Much of Campania is volcanic. Arriving by air, you look down on a dramatic landscape scarred with the escarpments and basins of old craters. It still leaks steam at the seams and is shaken from time to time by tremors, including one in 1980 that killed more than 2,000 people in the province. Vesuvius preserved for posterity the time-warp museum cities of Pompeii and Herculaneum by burying them in AD79. It last erupted in 1944, and hasn't finished yet.

Fiery Citizens

The people can be volcanic, too. A group on a street corner whose voices and gestures seem to verge on mayhem may just be having a friendly (albeit animated) chat. Neapolitan hand and body language can communicate hundreds of messages without words, and words without gestures in southern Italy would be like pasta without the sauce. The Neapolitan shrug – meaning anything from 'Who knows?' to 'What do you expect me to do about it?' – is the world's greatest shrug. This is some of the best people-watching in Italy, and that's saying something.

Negotiating the city is not as fraught with danger as some people, including Neapolitans, would have visitors believe. There are areas that are effectively no-go areas for tourists (the slum districts of Forcella and Ponticelli, for example), but most of Naples is no more threatening than any other major city.

The southerner's loyalty is to the family. On holidays, restaurants will be full of three- and four-generation family gatherings. At picnic spots a friendly stranger will often be invited to share. On Sundays young couples with chil-

Naples-speak

The local dialect is more like a language unto itself and can be incomprehensible to Italians from the North – or just about anywhere that is not Naples. The cadence is unique, word endings tend to drop off and diminutives are added to everything. Naples' rich heritage under Spanish and French rule becomes obvious.

Having served (and outwitted) many foreign rulers, the working people of Naples and the surrounding region have evolved a practice of flattery that is totally tongue-in-cheek. Almost any reasonably well-dressed male adult will be called 'dottore' (ie, a person with a university degree, not a doctor of medicine). A little grey hair will earn the title 'professore'. Locally, a man of power and/or dignity may be addressed as 'don', a tradition from the Spanish era. Unfortunately, none of the above can always be taken to imply genuine respect, given the Neapolitan's penchant for a cynical nature.

dren will be seen carrying neatly packaged pastries and bunches of flowers on their way to visit *la nonna* – Grandma. Graves are regularly tended and decorated with flowers, as are street corner shrines that are often dedicated to a departed parent. Many a family is supported by the remittances of a member working in Turin or Brooklyn.

A shrine in the Spanish Quarter

Unemployment in the Mezzogiorno ('Midday'), as the South is known, is almost twice the national average. Naples itself is haunted by a violent history and tattered trappings of bygone glory. These days, when the city is most notorious for poverty, crime, congestion and inefficient services, when its sons and daughters leave home to find work in the North and abroad, the proud claim *Vide Napoli e poi morí* – 'See Naples and die' – has a sardonic rather than a boastful ring.

But much is to be considered before accepting the stereotype of what the people of the Bay of Naples are supposed to be. Consider, too, the amazing history that has flowed and settled over Naples and its environs. Instead of a freeze-frame of a moment in the past, as captured in Pompeii, this is a living, brawling family, proud of its genealogy and its heirlooms, still growing, hospitable, but struggling to make ends meet, in a way that is unique to the Neapolitans.

A BRIEF HISTORY

Naples' history begins in the 8th century BC, when Greek colonists established a settlement on the Pizzofalcone hill and named it after the siren Parthenope. It became an important trading post in the Mediterranean and over the course of a century developed into a model Greek city. The Greeks gradually gained control of the whole region and founded Neapolis nearby. By 400BC the 'new city' had become the thriving commercial and intellectual capital of Campania, the northernmost province of Magna Graecia.

Meanwhile the Romans were busy expanding their own empire and in 326BC they conquered Naples. Soon almost the entire Italian peninsula was under their control. Impressed by what the Greeks had achieved, the Romans absorbed and adapted much of the Hellenic culture. During the 1st century AD, the bay area became fashionable among wealthy and aristocratic Romans, who built holiday homes and health spas. Emperor Nero had a beachside residence in Baia. Roman poets Ovid, Virgil and Horace were drawn to the south, inspired by its landscapes and the remnants of Greek culture. Pompeii and Herculaneum were two such thriving towns until they were buried by the eruption of Vesuvius in AD79.

After the Imperial capital was moved from Rome to Byzantium in 330, and the empire divided into east and west, Germanic tribes poured into Italy. The Goths sacked Rome in 410 and ravaged all Campania. There was more of the same from the Vandals in 455. Emperor Romulus Augustulus fled to Naples,

Imperial residence

Emperor Tiberius built a huge villa on the isle of Capri from where, between orgies, he ruled the Roman Empire for 10 years.

where he died in 476 leaving no successor. Thus, the Western Roman Empire effectively came to an end in Naples.

In due course, the Eastern Roman Empire of Byzantium allowed Naples to elect its own Dux (duke). The city became rich: churches and houses were built, art and culture flourished.

South of Naples, another coastal town was prospering. In the 9th century, Amalfi emerged as an independent merchant republic. But while Naples and Amalfi thrived, the rest of the south had been left exhausted and vulnerable – easy prey for the Germanic Lombards who had been busy rampaging across northern Italy. Over the next decades control of the south was divided between Byzantine rulers and the Lombards.

Pompeiian finds illustrate the Romans' luxurious lifestyle

Normans and Germans

In the 11th century, Norman crusaders returning from Palestine started to settle in southern Italy. A century later, Byzantine rule had been eliminated and most of southern Italy was under Norman control. Overall the Norman period of rule was one of relative peace and prosperity. But the stability of the region was shaken in 1189 by the death of William II, King of Sicily, and the ensuing power struggle between his bastard cousin Tancred and Henry VI of Hohenstaufen.

Henry finally conquered the Sicilian Kingdom and Naples in 1194. The Neapolitan people showed little liking for their new monarch, but their hostility changed to enthusiasm under the rule of his son Frederick II. Born and bred at the crossroads of the Byzantine, Arab and Norman cultures, Frederick was tolerant in his politics. His court in Palermo became a centre for writers, artists and scientists. Frederick also did great things for Naples. He completed the Castel Capuano and Castel dell'Ovo and founded the University of Naples.

After Frederick's death in 1251, Hohenstaufen rule disintegrated. In 1268 Charles of Anjou, brother of the French king Louis IX, took control of the Kingdom of Naples and Sicily and set up his court at Naples. The Angevin kings were keen to re-establish Naples as a cultural capital and during their period of rule a wealth of churches and monuments were built, including the Castel Nuovo, the monastery of San Martino, the cathedral and Santa Chiara church. Robert the Wise, the most powerful of the Angevin rulers, filled his court at Castel Nuovo with theologians, scientists, astrologers, monks and artists, Giotto among them. The Angevins maintained control one way or another until 1435, a period punctuated by Sicilian rebellion and a protracted, desultory war with the Aragons of Spain.

Charles of Anjou set up his court in Naples in 1268

Spanish Viceroys

During the late 15th and early 16th centuries the Italian peninsula was in a constant state of turmoil, first through bloody rivalry between France and Spain, and then in the battles to repulse

The baroque Palazzo Reale, built under Spanish rule

Turkish invasions. Naples was a pawn in these struggles. Spanish rule gained a strong foothold in 1504, when King Ferdinand of Spain (the sponsor of Columbus) made his military chief, Gonzalo de Cordoba, 'El Gran Capitan,' viceroy in Naples. There followed a succession of some 60 viceroys until 1734. Pedro de Toledo, viceroy from 1532–1553, cleaned up the city, installing sewers, pushing back the walls and carving out the central boulevard that bears his name today.

Perhaps because of Spanish clericalism, the humanising spirit of the Renaissance was slow to arrive in Naples; at the same time, however, the tolerant Neapolitans prevented the Spanish Inquisition from taking hold. Spain's artistic influence can be seen in the baroque architecture of many of the churches and palaces, including the magnificent Palazzo Reale and a (then) new university that now houses the National Museum.

The viceroys ruled as absolute monarchs and exacted heavy taxes on everything that came and went through the city gates. In 1647, discontented Neapolitan liberals engineered an uprising, ostensibly led by a fisherman named Tommaso Aniello (known as Masaniello), who proclaimed the Parthenopean Republic, with himself *generalissimo*. This was going too far for his backers. Masaniello was assassinated and the revolt was quashed the following year. Then in 1656 the unhappy city was hit by a plague that carried off around 400,000 people in six months.

All Europe became embroiled in the War of the Spanish Succession (1701–14) to decide whether French Bourbon or Austrian Habsburg claimants should take the vacant throne in Spain. Philip V, a Bourbon, was crowned in Madrid, but in the treaties ending the war Naples passed to Habsburg Austria. Viceroys appointed by Austria proceeded to govern the city until 1734, when Philip's son Charles chased them out and entered Naples to wild rejoicing as Charles III. The first of the Bourbon kings of Naples and Sicily, his realm comprised the lower half of the Italian boot, Sicily, Sardinia and the smaller islands. He built splendid palaces at Caserta and Capodimonte, as well as the prestigious San Carlo opera house. His Naples was a brilliant capital, a thriving port, and one of the largest cities of Europe.

Artistic riches

Charles III brought to Naples one of Europe's finest collections of art and antiquities, and added further to it by supporting the first excavations of Pompeii and other sites.

Revolution and Unification

Charles's successor Ferdinand IV had to flee to Sicily in 1806, when Napoleon sent an army to put his brother Joseph on the throne of Naples. Two years later Napoleon promoted Joseph to be King of Spain and replaced him in Naples with his brother-in-law, Joachim Murat. The English fleet took Capri briefly and bombarded Ischia.

After the fall of Napoleon and Murat, Ferdinand was restored to power, this time as Ferdinand I of the Kingdom of the Two Sicilies. Three more Bourbon kings followed – Francesco I, Ferdinand II, and Francesco II – all noted for their misrule and their complete disregard of the changes sweeping Europe. In 1848 Ferdinand II responded to agitation for more democracy by creating a constitutional parliament and then throwing its leading members in jail. These events prompted Prime Minister Gladstone's famous condemnation of the Bourbon regime as 'the negation of God erected into a system of government'.

Giuseppe Garibaldi, 'the father of modern Italy'

When Giuseppe Garibaldi landed in Sicily in May 1860 with his One Thousand (fighters for Italian unification), he had no difficulty in defeating the Bourbon troops, and his own small army grew as it rapidly advanced toward Naples. Francesco II, king for barely a year, fled as the city turned out *en masse* to welcome Garibaldi. A plebiscite overwhelmingly approved the union of Naples and Sicily with the new Kingdom of Italy under King Vittorio Emanuele II of Savoy.

The 20th Century

Under Mussolini the south of Italy was a place of exile, something of an Italian Siberia. In 1943, during World War

II, Allied armies landed at Salerno. Naples was bombed frequently, and upon departure the retreating German army burned the ancient archives of the city. The harbour, packed with ships protected by barrage balloons, became an important supply link for the Allied forces – and a bonanza for Neapolitan smugglers and black marketeers. Caserta became the Allied headquarters. While Mussolini and the Germans held Rome and the north of Italy, the south joined the Allies as a 'co-belligerent' under Marshall Badoglio. After the war, traditionally monarchist Naples voted against the creation of the Republic of Italy.

In an effort to alleviate the poverty of the region the *Cassa per il Mezzogiorno*, the Fund for the South, was created during the 1950s. Factories, steel mills and power plants were built, the *autostrada* network of roads was extended, swampy lands were drained, and agricultual methods became significantly modernised. However, many of the attempts at industrialisation have failed. The worldwide decline in shipping has reduced the commerical importance of the port.

The ancient criminal brotherhood, the Camorra, older than the Mafia, has recently been revived, and thrives on rackets and the drug trade. Fighting between rival factions led to a number of murders in late 2006, although the violence was mainly confined to the suburbs.

New Year fireworks display

Nevertheless, hopes for the future are high. Many predict tourism to be the major growth industry for Naples, its coast and its enchanting hinterland, as it was in the days of the Grand Tour.

Historical Landmarks

8th century BC Greeks establish a colony at Parthenope.

474BC Greeks found the new city of Neapolis near Parthenope.

4th century BC Neapolis is commercial capital of Campania.

326BC Rome conquers Neapolis

AD26 Emperor Tiberius rules the Roman Empire from Capri.

AD79 Vesuvius erupts destroying Pompeii and Herculaneum.

476 Last Roman emperor, Romulus Augustulus, dies in Naples.

763 Naples becomes a duchy.

9th century Amalfi becomes a thriving independent republic.

1139 Naples falls to the Normans.

1194 Henry VI of Germany becomes King of Naples.

1266 Kingdom of Naples given to the French Royal House of Anjou.

1442 Alfonso of Aragon conquers Naples and unites it with Sicily.

1495 Charles VII of France conquers Naples and reigns briefly.

1503 Spain defeats France, rules Naples for two centuries.

1647 People's revolt led by a Neapolitan fisherman violently quashed.

1688 Large parts of the city destroyed by an earthquake.

1707 The Austrian Habsburgs gain control of Naples.

1738 Austria loses Naples and Sicily to the Spanish Bourbons.

1806–15 Napoleon briefly controls Naples.

1859–60 Italian War of Liberation, led by Giuseppe Garibaldi. Naples becomes part of unified Kingdom of Italy.

1880–1914 More than 2.5 million Italians emigrate to the Americas.

1943 Naples bombed by Allied forces. After a four-day uprising by the people the German occupying troops withdraw from the city.

1980 Campania struck by earthquake; 3,000 killed.

2000 Rosa Russo Jervolino elected as Naples' first woman mayor.

2002 The lira is replaced by the euro.

2005 Opening of two new art centres, MADRE and PAN *(see pages 34 and 27 respectively)*, in Naples.

2006 Romano Prodi's centre-left coalition wins general election. Italy win the FIFA World Cup. Camorra infighting breaks out in Naples' suburbs.

WHERE TO GO

One of the great advantages of visiting Naples and its region is that its many different points of interest for art, history, scenic beauty and leisure are within easy reach of each other and well connected by excellent public transport. You don't have to choose between seeing Sorrento or Pompeii, or dining alfresco above Naples' harbour. You can do them all in a single day if you want – although travellers soon find themselves succumbing to a more relaxed southern-Italian approach to sightseeing, particularly in summer heat that can be as steamy as the city's trademark volcano. If you want to rush around the sights it is advisable to visit in winter or early spring.

Naples and the Neapolitans make up a fascinating, chaotic urban organism; the city itself is a brilliant living museum. Discovering its treasures is an adventure that leads from the famous bay to the heights, through hectic traffic and narrow byways where noisy family life spills out on to the streets. Even tourists looking forward to relaxing at one of the seaside resorts or islands shouldn't miss the Naples experience.

Come prepared to walk, for whether you're in Old Naples, older Pompeii, or even older Paestum, this is the way to enter the vibrant spirit of the place. The following itineraries are designed to help you discover this spirit for yourself.

NAPLES

A four-lane, one-way boulevard ceaselessly humming with traffic skirts an arc of the photogenic seafront west to east, from the bustling ferry docks of Mergellina to the headland of Pizzofalcone where the Greeks laid the foundations of a new town, Neapolis, nearly 3,000 years ago. At the foot of the hill, just off a little peninsula at the centre of the horseshoe-shaped bay, stands the islet fortress of **Castel dell'Ovo** (open Mon–Sat 8am–6pm, Sun 8am–2pm; free), Naples' oldest castle and a good place to begin exploring.

The tiny islet on which the castle now stands was originally used by the Greeks as a harbour. Later, the Roman general Lucullus had a villa on Pizzofalcone and built an annexe on the rocks offshore, where he used to store food and wine for his legendary banquets. In the 5th century, a monastery was built here, then in the 12th century, it was transformed into a fort by the Normans. The present structure dates from the early 16th century, following its near destruction by the Spanish. Today, the rooms of the castle are closed except when they are used for cultural events and exhibitions, but you can wander around the battlements and enjoy views across the bay.

In the shadow of the castle is a small harbour filled with pleasure craft and little fishing boats. The docks and castle walls

Naples' oldest castle, the island fortress Castel dell'Ovo

are lined with seafood restaurants and cafés. This compact area, known as **Borgo Marinaro**, is the hub of the **Santa Lucia** district. The former fishing community, hailed in the quintessential Neapolitan song, is now an obligatory port of call for the hungry tourist and a good place to sample authentic fish dishes.

A good egg

Castel dell'Ovo gets its name from the egg (ovo) supposedly buried in its foundations. The poet Virgil, who was thought to possess powers of divination, warned that if the egg ever broke catastrophe would befall the city.

Opposite the Castel dell' Ovo, the sea-facing Via Partenope is a row of the city's grandest and most historic hotels – the Vesuvio, Santa Lucia and Excelsior all offer splendid views of the bay and Vesuvius. From the elegant seafront, walk down Via Santa Lucia, which edges the much scruffier back streets of the working class Palinotto district.

Royal Naples

At the end of Via Santa Lucia, turn left into Via C Console which opens out into the **Piazza del Plebiscito**. The vast semicircular square was used for decades as a car park, but it was cleared of traffic during the 1990s clean-up campaign and is now the domain of energetic children, dogs and strollers. The piazza commemorates the incorporation of the Kingdom of the Two Sicilies into the Italian national state in 1860, an event which resulted in Naples losing its traditional function as a capital. It is dominated on one side by the Palazzo Reale (Royal Palace) and on the other by the domed church of San Francesco di Paola.

The grimly imposing **Palazzo Reale** (open Thur–Tues 9am–7pm; palace: admission fee, courtyard and gardens: free) was built by Spanish viceroys in the early 17th century, but it takes its character from the sojourn of the Bourbon

San Francesco di Paola was modelled on the Pantheon in Rome

monarchs and of Joachim Murat who lived here during his short reign as king of Naples with his wife, Napoleon's sister, Caroline Bonaparte. The Savoy king Umberto I installed the statues on the facade. From left to right, they are the Norman Roger I, Frederick II of Hohenstaufen, Charles I of Anjou, Alfonso I of Aragon, the Habsburg–Spanish emperor Charles V, Charles III of Bourbon, Murat and Vittorio Emanuele II of Savoy.

The palace was badly damaged by Allied bombs in 1943 and by the occupying forces. When the Italian government recovered it, the royal apartments had to be refurbished. They are now arranged as a museum with paintings and period furniture brought from various sources. The palace is also home to the **Biblioteca Nazionale** (open Mon–Fri 8.30am–7.30pm, Sat 8.30am–1.30pm; free with ID card), the largest public library in southern Italy. Among its treasures are a 1485 copy of Dante's *Divine Comedy* illustrated with Botticelli engravings; illuminated medieval manuscripts; and most of the priceless papyri found in Herculaneum in 1752 *(see page 59)*.

Opposite the palace, the massive church of **San Francesco di Paola** was built in 1817 and modelled on the Pantheon in Rome. Outside, are two equestrian statues of Ferdinand IV and his father, Charles III of Bourbon, both by Canova.

Backing on to the Palace on Piazza Trieste e Trento is the **Teatro di San Carlo** (open daily for tours 9am–5.30pm; admission charge; opera season from Nov or Dec–May, but with concerts all year; <www.teatrosancarlo.it>), Italy's most prestigious opera house after La Scala in Milan and the oldest continuously performing opera house in Europe. It was built for Charles III in 1737 in just eight months and rebuilt after a fire in 1816. Though sombre outside, the rich red-and-gold hall interior is dazzling. Rossini, Donizetti, Bellini and Verdi all composed operas for San Carlo. The ticket office is opposite in the cavernous, glass-roofed **Galleria Umberto I**. It was a showcase when it was completed in 1890. Today it is lined with a number of shops and cafés, but remains strangely empty despite the crowded streets outside.

Diagonally opposite the theatre is the lavish *belle époque* **Gran Caffè Gambrinus**, worth visiting for a coffee and cake or an early evening aperitif. Once the haunt of writers and artists, it's a perfect, if noisy spot for people-watching.

Underground tours

Gran Caffè Gambrinus is the starting point for one of several fascinating walking tours of subterranean Naples, which take in a mix of secret tunnels, catacombs, underground aqueducts, air raid shelters, archaeological remnants of the ancient city, the new metro, beautifully adorned in art, and of course, plenty of ghosts. There is a whole different world down there, not to be missed. Advance booking essential, tel: 081-296 944, <www.lanapolisotterranea.it>.

Castel Nuovo, begun in 1279

Port and Castel Nuovo

Heading east along Via Vittorio Emanuele, you'll come to the second castle in our itinerary, standing guard over Naples' harbour. Giant cruise ships dock at the Stazione Marittima while smaller ferries and hydrofoils that ply between Sorrento and the islands flow in and out of the adjacent Molo Beverello. The **Castel Nuovo** (open Mon–Sat 9am–7pm, Sun 9am–2pm; admission fee) – the 'New' Castle of 1279, as opposed to the old Castel dell'Ovo – is commonly called the Maschio Angioino, the Angevin Fortress, because it was begun by Charles I of Anjou. Sandwiched between two of the five grim, grey towers is the ornate white Triumphal Arch commissioned by Alfonso of Aragon in 1442, to commemorate his defeat of the French and entry into Naples. Across the courtyard, the Palatine chapel is all that remains of the original 13th-century structure. The staircase in the far corner leads to the Hall of the Barons featuring a spectacular rib-vaulted ceiling (now the City Council Chamber).

Spread across two upper floors, the **Museo Civico** displays a collection of silver and bronze artefacts and paintings from the 15th to the 20th centuries. Note also the tablet commemorating the uprising of September 1943, when the Germans were expelled from Naples.

Chiaia

To the right of Piazza del Plebiscito, behind Caffè Gambrinus, **Via Chiaia** skirts the Pizzofalcone hill. This street, lined with boutiques, leads to the elegant **Piazza dei Martiri** and the wealthy district of Chiaia, home to stylish but pricy shops, art galleries and antiques dealers, which spread into its side-streets.

A short walk towards the bay leads to the congested **Piazza Vittoria** (commemorating the defeat of the Turkish fleet at Lepanto in 1571) and the entrance to the 1.5-km (1-mile) long **Villa Comunale**. All Naples comes to stroll or sit in this leafy seafront park on Sundays and summer evenings. In the park, Europe's oldest **Aquarium** (open Tues–Sat 9am–4.30pm; Sun 9.30am–1.30pm; admission fee) is looking its age. It was founded in 1872 by the German naturalist Anton Dohrn. Inside are 200 species of marine life from the Bay of Naples.

The promenade on the sea side of the park following the *lungomare* (Via Caracciolo), is one of Italy's most panoramic, if you can ignore the traffic and fumes. Parallel to this, on the far side of the park, is the fashionable **Riviera di Chiaia**, once popular with English visitors on the Grand Tour.

Halfway down the broad avenue, lined with grand 19th-century *palazzi*, stands the **Villa Pignatelli** (open Tues–Sun 8.30am–1.30pm; admission fee). The neoclassical villa was built in 1826 for Ferdinand Acton, son of Ferdinand IV's prime minister, John Acton. The museum has a collection of porcelain and paintings, books and music recordings, and a score of late 19th-century carriages.

Palace of Art

Set in a stunning 17th-century building, the Palazzo delle Arti Napoli (PAN; Via dei Mille 60; open Mon, Wed–Sat 9.30am–7.30pm, Sun and hols 9.30am–2.30pm; admission fee; <www.palazzoarti napoli.net>), just north of Chiaia, is a dazzling art gallery with exhibitions, cultural activities and cutting edge contemporary art.

The park's western end is bounded by Piazza della Repubblica which marks the beginning of the Mergellina district. From here, palazzo-lined Viale Gramsci leads to the chaotic Piazza Sannazzaro and the port of **Mergellina**. *Aliscafi* (hydrofoils) leave from here for the islands and Sorrento. Just beyond the port is a little park lined with good seafood restaurants, less touristy than those of Santa Lucia. Posillipo's hills come close to the seafront here *(see page 43)*.

Centro Storico

The gateway to Old Naples is the shop-lined **Via Toledo**, laid out by the Spanish Viceroy at the edge of the old city in 1536. The lower end as far as Piazza Carità is pedestrianised. Opposite the Galleria Umberto's western entrance, is a station for one of the three funiculars to the hilltop Vomero district *(see page 41)*. Flanking the left-hand side is a labyrinth of tiny streets that make up the **Quartiere Spagnoli**, where soldiers were billeted during the centuries of Spanish rule. Today it is still shaking off its reputation as a den of petty crime. The mere mention of the Spanish Quarter conjures images of Vespa-riding purse-snatchers who disappear with their loot into the narrow alleys and staircase streets of this crowded district of tenements. Things have improved in recent years but tourists should enter with caution and without valuables.

From Via Toledo, turn right down Via Armando Diaz, planted with orange trees. A typical example of the architecture of Mussolini's fascist era is the Central Post Office in Piazza Matteotti, built in 1925. In contrast, at the head of the Via Monteoliveto around the corner, is the 16th-century Renaissance Florentine facade of **Palazzo Gravina**, now the university's School of Architecture.

Across the street from the Palazzo Gravina in Piazza Monteoliveto, is the plain, grey **Sant'Anna dei Lombardi**. The Piccolomini Chapel to the left of the entrance holds two fine

Giovanni Vasari's ceiling in Sant'Anna dei Lombardi

works by Florentine artist Antonio Rosselino – a 1475 marble nativity with lively angels dancing on the stable roof, and the tomb of Maria d'Aragona, a masterpiece of classic sobriety. In the chapel to the right of the altar is Guido Mazzoni's *Pietà* (1492), a remarkably modelled group of eight life-sized terracotta figures. On the right at the rear of the church, the stalls of the old sacristy are beautifully backed with early 16th-century *intarsia* work, designs in inlaid wood.

At the end of Calata Trinità Maggiore, the Jesuit church known as the **Gesù Nuovo** (open daily 7am–12.30pm, 4–7.30pm) in the piazza of the same name, is effectively the centre of the old city. The unusual diamond-point facade belonged to a 15th-century princely palace and does not prepare you for the opulent blaze of overblown baroque gold within. The decorative spire in the piazza is a *guglia* (one of three in Naples old town) Naples' characteristically flamboyant answer to the obelisks of Rome.

Baroque refits

Naples has almost 400 churches. Regardless of when they were built, they tend to look alike, since most of them were redecorated in the florid baroque style.

Spaccanapoli

The ancient Greek street that crosses the Piazza del Gesù Nuovo has six names along its arrow-straight 5-km (3-mile) east–west course (Via Benedetto Croce and Via San Biagio are the two most prominent) but is best known as **Spaccanapoli**, literally 'Split-Naples'. The Spaccanapoli district has been at the heart of Naples since Greek and Roman times. A walk along its length, wandering off into side alleys and squares, is the quintessential Neapolitan experience. Half-doors, with the upper part open, reveal the tidy interiors of *bassi*, windowless one- or two-room street-level apartments in the 19th-century buildings, each of which may be home to a large family. Doorways and the street become an extension of the *bassi* where family members sit on chairs peeling vegetables, playing cards and conversing in explosive bursts of dialect.

Just beyond the Piazza del Gesù Nuovo, to the right, looms **Santa Chiara** (open daily 7.30am–1pm, 4–8pm; museum open Mon–Sat 9.30am–6.30pm, Sun 9.30am–2.30pm; admission fee). Its soaring Provençal Gothic nave is a magnificent relic of Angevin Naples, completed in 1328. It, too, was covered with baroque plaster and gilt in the 18th century. After American bombs caused a two-day fire that gutted the church in 1943 (and destroyed what is believed to have been a cycle of frescoes by Giotto), the rediscovered underlying Gothic lines were kept in the post-war restoration. Fortunately the bombs spared the glorious 14th-century frescoed cloisters, with 18th-century painted majolica tiles, one of the city's most tranquil and photogenic spots.

A little further along is **Piazza San Domenico Maggiore**. Its *guglia* (obelisk) commemorates the terrible plague of

1656, which carried off half the population. In the 13th century St Thomas Aquinas lived and taught in the convent attached to **San Domenico Maggiore** (open daily 8.30am–noon, 4.30–7pm; treasury open Sat 9.30am–noon, 4.30–7pm, Sun 9.30am–noon; admission fee), one of the largest churches in Naples, with a supposedly miraculous crucifix. The treasury, built to house the hearts of the Aragonese kings who are buried here now houses many royal religious artifacts.

Turn left at the square, past the imposing portal of the Palazzo di Sangro, and right into Via F. de Sanctis to find the **Cappella Sansevero** (open Mon, Wed–Sat 10am–5.40pm, Sun and hols 10am–1.10pm; admission fee) the private chapel and burial place of the noble di Sangro family, the Princes of Sansevero. In the 18th century Prince Raimondo, a soldier and obsessive alchemist, had the 16th-century chapel lavishly redecorated. In the crypt are two skeletons meshed in metal

The exquisite frescoes of Santa Chiara's tranquil cloisters

A card game on Via dei Tribunali

veins. They are thought to be the bodies of servants the eccentric Raimondo experimented on. But the reason most people visit the chapel is to see the beautifully carved alabaster figure of the *Veiled Christ* (1753), a masterpiece by Giuseppe Sammartino.

Running parallel to Spaccanapoli is **Via dei Tribunali**, flanked by an ancient arcade. In the morning the street is a bustling market, with housewives delving into buckets of fish and vendors displaying produce in stalls that offer the day's best buys from the rich Campanian fields.

Here you'll find the medieval church of **San Lorenzo Maggiore** (open Mon–Sat 7.45am–7.15pm, Sun 7.48am–1pm, 5–7.15pm; museum open Mon–Sat 9.30am–5.30pm, Sun 9.30am–1.30pm; admission fee) and its 17th-century cloister, set back on a platform on the right, where excavations have uncovered parts of the Roman law courts and, below that, Greek shops and workshops of ancient Neapolis. The church has been restored to the Gothic of the French architects who built the luminous ribbed apse in the late 1200s. Its showpiece is the 14th-century tomb of Catherine of Austria by Tino di Camaino, one of the first and finest Gothic sculptors in Italy.

Linking Via Dei Tribunali with Spaccanapoli (at Via San Biagio dei Librai) is **Via San Gregorio Armeno**. This little street is crammed with dozens of shops selling figurines and knick-knacks for Christmas cribs *(presepi)*. Amidst the recent inundation of mass-produced, poor quality merchandise, a knowing eye can still ferret out the best – hand-made items that will amaze and delight you with their attention to minute detail.

The cloister of the adjoining convent of **San Gregorio Armeno** (open Mon–Sat 9am–noon, Sun 9am–1pm), with its fountain and orange trees, offers a place of refuge.

The Duomo

North of Via dei Tribunali, on Via del Duomo is the cathedral of San Gennaro, or **Duomo** (open Mon–Sat 8.30am–12.30pm, 4.30–7pm, Sun and hols 8.30am–1pm, 5–7pm; free; archaeological area and baptistry open Mon–Sat 9am–noon, 4.30–7pm, Sun 9am–noon, treasury open Tues–Sun 9.30am–5pm; admission fee). The cathedral is a none too harmonious mixture of styles dating back to pre-Christian times – there are more than 100 Greek and Roman granite columns incorporated in the 16 piers of its nave. The first Angevin king, Charles I, began the cathedral in 1272 on the site of a 5th-century church that in turn had replaced a Roman temple.

The oldest portion is actually another church, Santa Restituta, on a lower level entered from the left aisle. This 4th-

Chiuso

Chiuso (pronounced 'kyoo-zo') is a word you'll learn soon after *grazie* and *per favore*. It means closed. Closed for lunch, closed by a strike, closed 'temporarily' for repairs for many years, closed for whatever reasons and however long. Be prepared every day to find something you hoped to see *chiuso*. Numerous rooms in the National Museum have been closed for years; others, and not always the same ones, are closed in the afternoons when the rest of the museum is open. Landmark churches listed on the Naples Tourist Bureau itinerary of artistic monuments are padlocked, or open only a few hours a day. The Blue Grotto is *chiuso* when wind whips up the waves, closing the narrow entrance. Most petrol stations are *chiuso* on Monday; some that say *aperto* (open) are unstaffed and effectively *chiuso* unless you know how to operate the money machines.

The Duomo

century basilica, the oldest Christian building in Naples, retains 5th-century mosaics in the domed baptistery and notable 13th-century marble reliefs in the side chapels. The church was redesigned a number of times, following the disastrous earthquakes of 1349 and 1456. Its massive 1407 doors were incorporated into the present facade, finished in 1905.

Naples has endured so many catastrophes that the populace could be excused for doubting the protective powers of its patron saint, San Gennaro. However, on the right side of the cathedral, the **Cappella di Tesoro** (Treasury Chapel) enshrines the relics of the city's revered patron. On the first Sunday of May and on 19 September, his feast day, two small phials of his coagulated blood (kept in an elaborate silver reliquary) are said to miraculously liquefy. If the blood does not liquefy, disaster is said to strike. The last time the saint did not cooperate was in 1980 – when Vesuvius erupted.

Just north of the cathedral, in Palazzo Donnaregina on Via Settembrini 79, the **Museo d'Arte Donna Regina** (MADRE; open Mon, Wed, Thur, Sun 10am–9pm, Fri–Sat 10am–midnight; admission fee, free Mon) is a shock after all the baroque. Housed within a former convent, this modern art gallery is worth a visit, not least for the architecture by Alvaro Siza, successfully marrying the historic and the contemporary.

Around Corso Umberto I

As Via del Duomo descends toward the harbour it crosses the Corso Umberto I, one of the city's major arteries. Three blocks past the intersection, Via Giubbonari passes under a Gothic clock tower into the **Piazza del Mercato**, home of the church of **Santa Maria del Carmine** (open Mon–Sat 7am–noon, 4.45–7.30pm, Sun 7am–1pm, 4.30–7.30pm).

The market square is laden with history. An executioner's block for condemned nobles and a gallows for commoners were kept here for centuries. Its principal fame dates back to 1647 when the fisherman Tommaso Aniello, 'Masaniello', began the revolt of the first Parthenopean Republic here. It ended when he was shot nearby. The liberals who proclaimed the abortive second republic in 1799 were executed here, too. Thousands of victims of the 17th-century plague were buried in a common grave under the pavement. The church, already in existence in the 12th century, has a special place in the hearts of Neapolitans. A much venerated 14th-century image of the dark-haired Madonna, 'la Bruna', is enshrined here. On 15 July the bell tower erupts in a shower of fireworks, to simulate the one-time burning of the narrow campanile.

The most colourful outdoor fish market in Naples sprawls along Via Carmignano, beginning behind the church. It's a vibrant, quintessentially Neapolitan scene. Hoses spray octopi to keep them wriggling, crustaceans of all sizes struggle to escape from their baskets, and the haggling of shoppers competes with the cries of vendors in a street-opera din. The street follows the line of old city walls. Through the arch and across the Rettifilo, street stalls of the Forcella market spill over into the alleys around Via Forcella.

Black-market goods

Forcella is the Naples 'thieves' market', famous during World War II as the clearing house for loot and contraband lifted from the Allied forces.

Like the Corso Umberto I, **Piazza Garibaldi** is a product of the *sventramento*, the 19th-century 'disembowelling' of Old Naples in the interests of sanitation and urban planning. Nevertheless, the district around the main station has something of a reputation for hustlers and pickpockets. The **Stazione Centrale** is the terminus of trains from Rome and of a metro that runs on the same track. The Circumvesuviana line serves Vesuvius, Pompeii, Herculaneum and Sorrento. There is a tourist information office on the upper concourse.

A handsome remnant of the old city walls, the **Porta Capuana**, adorns the Piazza Capuana northwest of Piazza Garibaldi. Buses leave every 20 minutes from here for the Royal Palace of Caserta, the Versailles of Italy *(see page 48)*.

Archaeological Museum

The upper levels of Naples possess three important museums, a fort, parks, and private villas with sweeping views of the city and bay. Begin halfway up, at the **Museo Archeologico Nazionale** (open Wed–Mon 9am–7.30pm; admission fee) at the northern edge of the Centro Storico, next to Piazza Cavour.

This museum's unsurpassed collection of antiquities encompasses the best of the treasures found at the Pompeii, Herculaneum and Phlegraean Fields sites, as well as the legendary Farnese collection of Roman statues that Charles III of Bourbon inherited from his mother, Elisabetta Farnese. So unexcelled were its wonders, it became an obligatory stop on any 18th-century traveller's Grand Tour. There's a huge amount to see, and it isn't made easier by the ongoing restoration programme. Visitors have to contend with the constant rearrangement of galleries and unexpected room closures.

The ground floor is mostly devoted to Roman copies of the work of the greatest sculptors of ancient Greece. The famous **Tyrannicides**, striding to strike, are in fact copies of a copy made in Athens in 440BC to replace the original, taken by

Persians. The undisputed highlights of the Farnese collection are the powerful **Hercules** and the grandiose **Farnese Bull**. The latter, miraculously carved out of a single massive block of marble, depicts the legend of Dirce, tied to a bull by Antiope's sons as punishment for trying to murder their mother. Both monumental statues were found in the 16th-century excavations of the Baths of Caracalla in Rome.

The displays on the mezzanine floor are centred on the finest mosaics and paintings from Pompeii. Exceptional is the large **Battle of Issus** from the House of the Dancing Faun. Alexander the

Treasures from Pompeii in the Archaeological Museum

Great charges bare-headed from the left as Persian soldiers try to turn the horses of Darius's chariot for flight. The original statue of the faun, after which the house was named, is here too. The Nile Scenes and detailed mosaics of marine creatures in the adjoining room are from the same house.

This is also the location of the Secret Cabinet or **Gabinetto Segreto**, opened to much fanfare in 1999. A manned gate leads to two rooms containing more than 200 frescoes, mosaics and explicit fertility symbols and statues. For decades these were kept hidden because they were deemed too pornographic for public viewing (a 2nd-century AD figure of Pan copulating with a goat could explain why).

One of the finest collections of classical sculptures

Upstairs, to the right, look for the treasures from the Villa of the Papyri in Herculaneum. This mansion and its garden were a veritable art gallery. The seated young Mercury was found there, together with the poised bronze racers and the row of muses that lined the garden pool.

Also on this floor is a series of rooms containing domestic items: lamps, mirrors, combs, theatre tickets, shoes, kitchenware, charred food, the instruments from Pompeii's House of the Surgeon, and the beautiful 115-piece silver service from the House of Menander. The top floor is given over to a hoard of Greek and Etruscan pottery, as well as the museum's collection of coins.

Just south of the museum is the recently finely restored **Galleria Principe de Napoli**, an architect's hymn of praise to shopping. Also nearby, the **Accademia di Belle Arti** (Via Santa Maria Costantinopoli; open Mon–Thur 10am–2pm, Fri 2–6pm; admission fee; <www.accademianapoli.it>) has a fine collection of 17th–20th century art. South of this on Via Santa Maria di Costantinopoli is the pretty Piazza Bellini, with its literary cafés and statue of the great composer. Beyond this, head through the covered Port d'Alba with its bookshops to **Piazza Dante**, an elegant but busy piazza at the end of Via Toledo, home to fast food, metro and bus termini.

The Catacombs and Capodimonte

Catch a bus uphill from the Museum or Piazza Dante to the **Catacombe di San Gennaro** (guided tours only, Tues–Sun, 9am, 10am, 11am, noon; admission fee). Get off at the domed Madre del Buon Consiglio church where the road doubles back sharply just below Capodimonte. The ticket booth for the catacombs is to the left of the church. The first tombs cut into the rock here were for pagan, 2nd-century Roman families of nobility. Use by Christians probably began a century or so later. The arched halls and rooms on two levels are decorated with very early mosaics and frescoes that date back to the 6th century.

Crowning the hill at the end of Via Capodimonte, in a vast shady park that once served as a royal hunting ground, is the **Museo Nazionale di Capodimonte** (open Thur–Tues 8.30am–7.30pm; admission fee), an oasis of calm and fresh

Il Canto Napolitano

Nostalgia and melancholy, sunshine and sea, love and betrayal are the hallmarks of songs that are as Neapolitan as pizza. The greatest Neapolitan singer of them all, Enrico Caruso, included *O sole mio!* and *Santa Lucia* in his concerts along with operatic arias, and made them familiar worldwide.

Neapolitan singing has an ancient pedigree. Night serenades became such a nuisance to the unromantic trying to sleep that King Frederick II issued a decree in 1221 banning the practice. In the 16th century Neapolitan ditties were popular all over Europe. In the 1700s and 1800s, comic operas flowed from Naples. Then café concerts became the rage. The festival of Santa Maria di Piedigrotta, a popular church in Mergellina, became a contest for new popular songs in 1876. First prize in 1880 went to *Funiculi, Funicula*, celebrating the funicular that had opened on Vesuvius. In 1878 *O sole mio!* won second prize of 200 lira. Even Elvis recorded that one.

air, away from the chaos of downtown Naples. The palace was built by Charles III in 1738 to house his picture collection. He also built the Capodimonte porcelain works in the grounds, its extravagantly ornate and delicate output becoming famous throughout Europe. There is plenty of porcelain still in the palace, whose sprawling chambers also house one of the finest picture galleries in southern Italy. On the first floor, the Farnese collection includes such masterpieces as Masaccio's *Crucifixion*, Botticelli's *Madonna and Child with Angels*, an early Renaissance treasure, *Antea* by Parmigianino, the portrait of a young elegantly dressed woman thought to be the artist's lover, and the monumental canvases by the Carraccis. Raphael is represented by his portraits of *Leo X and Two Cardinals* and *Cardinal Alessandro Farnese*. Pride of place is given to Titian's *Danaë* (1545).

Bellini's *Transfiguration of Christ* in the Capodimonte Museum

The **Galleria delle Cose Rare** contains a sparkling display of precious objects that once graced the Farnese palaces. The rooms beyond contain **Flemish paintings**, most of which were acquired by the Bourbons at the beginning of the 17th century when the Netherlands was enjoying an artistic golden age. Before proceeding to the second floor, wander through the ornate **Royal Apartments**, and marvel at the magnificent ballroom with its giant chandelier, and the Porcelain Parlour of Queen Maria Amalia, lined with over 3,000 tiles made in King Charles's porcelain factory.

The second floor is given over to Neapolitan art from the 13th to the 18th centuries. Among the early works is Simone Martini's *San Ludovico di Tolosa* (1317), a masterpiece of Italian Gothic art from San Lorenzo Maggiore. Central to the 17th-century works in the collection are the Caravaggio canvases, in particular the *Flagellation of Christ* (1607–10). The third floor is dedicated to modern and contemporary art. The star exhibit here is Andy Warhol's *Vesuvius*.

Vomero

The Vomero district is on another hill, reached from the seafront and centre of Naples by funicular. The three stations are at the foot of Via Toledo on the tiny Piazza Duca d'Aosta; on Piazza Montesanto across Via Toledo from the Piazza Dante; and in the Chiaia district at Piazza Amedeo. The Montesanto funicular comes closest to the Castel Sant'Elmo, but they all arrive within close walking distance of each other.

The hilltop citadel of Naples, the imposing **Castel Sant' Elmo** (open Thur–Tues 9am–6.30pm; admission fee) is a sombre and brooding presence when seen from below, but a breeze-swept platform for admiring the 360-degree view from its ramparts. Originally built in 1275, King Robert of Anjou enlarged the castle on this strategic spot in 1349, but its current form dates from the 16th century.

Just below the castle is the **Certosa e Museo di San Martino** (open Thur–Tues 8.30am–7.30pm; admission fee), a former Carthusian monastery and museum of Neapolitan history and culture. From the cloistered entry, proceed past the gold coach to the terraced gardens of vines, pines and paths. From this unique balcony *belvedere* you'll be able to identify the main landmarks of the city, spread out like a map below. To the right of the little cloister, the Maritime Section exhibits ship models. On the left, steps go down to the Presepe Cuciniello, the champion of all Neapolitan cribs. Each of the 177 painted terracotta figures is an exquisite work of art carved by the popular sculptor Giuseppe Sammartino, and clothed in handsewn period costumes. Rooms around the main cloister are devoted to the paintings of Neapolitan artists, costumes, glassware and historical exhibits.

The cloister is a restrained, rather Florentine construction, with a small monk's cemetery, guarded by skulls, in one corner. Continue through the chapter room of the monastery's church to see the fine *intarsia* (inlay) work on stalls and cabinets in the Sacristy and, in the Treasury Chapel, *Descent from the Cross*, one of the great masterpieces by José Ribera.

Three of 177 terracotta figures in San Martino's presepe

The monastery was founded in 1325 by Charles d' Anjou, but it was given a baroque makeover in the 16th and 17th centuries. Dozens of Neapolitan-school painters worked on these walls and on the side chapels, including Ribera, whose 12 prophets look out from over the chapel arches.

The Certosa di San Martino

The centre of the Vomero district is Piazza Vanvitelli, cut through from east to west by the shopping street of Via Scarlatti. The parallel street to the south is Via Cimarosa, where you'll find the **Parco della Floridiana** (open 9am–1hr before sunset), formerly the grounds of the 19th-century Villa Floridiana, now a public park. The royal summer palace now houses the **Museo Nazionale della Ceramica Duca di Martina** (guided tours only Wed–Mon 9.30am, 11am, 12.30pm; admission fee). In addition to the porcelain from the royal Capodimonte factory, this fine collection also has a valuable selection of Meissen, Sèvres, Nymphenburg, Wedgwood and Oriental ceramics and majolica.

Posillipo

Long before the Vomero district became fashionable, the seaside suburb of Posillipo, on the northern arm of the bay, was the retreat of the city's rich. Monte Posillipo, rimmed

The Posillipo peninsula was once such an idyllic rural landscape that the Greeks named it *Pausilypon* – 'the soothing of pain'. It is possible that Epicureanism, the philosophy based on the pursuit of pleasure, originated here.

with apartments and villas, slopes gently to the sea, closing the western end of the inner bay. The Via di Posillipo around this cape was begun by Murat in 1812 as a more direct route to Pozzuoli. This panoramic road follows the shore from Mergellina and climbs past parks and faded princely estates, such as the 17th-century **Palazzo di Donn'Anna** (privately owned). Passing a park with a World War I memorial, the road reaches a crest at the Quadrivio del Capo crossroads. Take the left road down about a kilometer (½ mile) to **Marechiaro**. Popular seafood and pizza restaurants ring the tiny harbour-side piazza of this former fishing village. Just beyond the Quadrivio, the Parco Virgiliano's belvedere offers splendid views over the bay out to Capri. Directly ahead, attached to the peninsula by a small strip of land, is the island of Nisida. Legend has it that Brutus and Cassius hatched their plot to kill Caesar here.

CAMPI FLEGREI

In the days of Imperial Rome the fashionable place to have a holiday villa was along the northern curve of the Bay of Naples, called the Phlegraean Fields (Campi Flegrei), from the Greek for 'burning fields.' The whole district overlies volcanic fire, dotted with hot springs and 13 small craters, one of which still shoots up clouds of sulphurous steam. Although stripped over the centuries and half buried by neglect and modern development, through the scattered remains you can still recreate the image of this ancient Roman playground in your mind's eye.

Pozzuoli

The busy town of Pozzuoli (pop. 70,000), 8km (5 miles) west of Naples, is the starting point for visiting the Phlegraean Fields sites. On a slope behind the harbour, the Duomo, the Cattedrale di San Procolo, was just another 17th-century church until a fire in 1964 uncovered the marble walls and cornices of a temple to Augustus, the first emperor to be deified. San Gennaro, Naples' patron saint, found early martyrdom here in AD305. These days, the town's most famous native is Sophia Loren, but it is also well known for its gastronomy.

Set back from the port area are the ruins of a 2nd-century BC *macellum* (market). These splendid ruins were submerged in water until the mid-1980s when the rising of land levels caused by volcanic activity left them uncovered.

The **Anfiteatro Flavio di Puteoli** (open Wed–Mon 9am–1hr before sunset; admission fee) is reached by steps and a

Pozzuoli harbour: beyond lie splendid Roman remains

A fisherman mends his nets

short street beyond the railway station opposite the harbour. It was covered by volcanic material until the 19th century and, as a result, is incredibly well preserved. Built in the 1st century AD, the amphitheatre held 35,000 spectators, and could be flooded for mock naval battles. About half an hour's walk uphill is the **Solfatara** (open daily 8.30am–1hr before dusk; admission fee), a shallow moonscape crater filled with glaring white ash. You are walking on top of a snoozing volcano, with the stink of sulphur in the air from steaming fumaroles and bubbling mud pits. At the Boca Grande fumarole, steam temperatures are over 160°C (320°F). This is where guides light a match at a vent, causing clouds of white ionised vapour to puff from cracks.

One of the newest museums in the bay area, the **Citta della Scienza** (open Mon–Sat 9am–5pm, Sun 10am–7pm, closed Mon in winter; admission charge) is in a stylishly converted industrial complex opposite Nisida island on the gulf of Pozzuoli. Billed as Italy's best hands-on science museum, it has a planetarium (Italian only) and some interesting displays, but probably not quite enough energy to keep the children captivated.

All along the Gulf of Pozzuoli out to its tip at Capo Miseno, Roman buildings that once stood on the shore are submerged, providing great treasure-hunting opportunities for divers.

Baia

The small seaside village of Baia was once a luxurious holiday resort for wealthy Romans. The **Parco Archeologico** (open Thur–Tues 9am–1hr before sunset) encloses the ruins of the Imperial Palace and baths, built and added to by the Caesars over 400 years from the 1st century AD. But signage is confusing, in typical Neapolitan style, and the entrance is virtually concealed. The easiest way is a footbridge over the tracks at the railway station. The site, on a cliff with three terrace levels, commands a view over the sea from Capo Miseno on the right, to Pozzuoli, Posillipo, Vesuvius and the Sorrento peninsula in the distance to the left. On the coast stood the villas of such illustrious Roman figures as Julius Caesar, Lucullus, Pompey, Cicero, Sulla – a veritable enclave of the rich and famous. Many of these villas are now under water (tours in glass-bottomed boats are available in summer); others provide walls for houses on the main street between the cliff and the bay. The whole complex was raided by Saracens in the 9th century.

Remains of Baia's ancient water supply system

After Baia the road climbs to the **Castello di Baia** (open Tues–Sun 9.15am–3.45pm; admission fee), a fortress that overlooks the Gulf of Pozzuoli, built by the Spanish to defend against the Saracensin the 16th century . The archaeological museum has finds from the Shrine of the Augustali at Miseno *(see page 48)* and a reconstruction of the submerged nymphaeum found at Epitaffio point, north of Baia port.

Descending to Bacoli, look for signs to the Piscina Mirabile. This vast covered reservoir carved out of the rock, the largest of its kind, was the terminus of an aqueduct designed to provide water for the Roman fleet at Miseno.

The sheltered harbour at **Capo Miseno** was used as a naval base first by the Greeks then by the Romans. Pliny the Elder was in command of the fleet here when Vesuvius erupted in AD79, and met his death trying to save fugitives from Pompeii. The famous description of the event by his nephew Pliny the

The Royal Palace at Caserta

Perhaps the most grandiose palace in all Italy lies 28km (18 miles) northeast of Naples. Charles III almost certainly had Versailles in mind when he set out in 1751 to create the Royal Palace of the Bourbons at Caserta. It was completed in 1774 by his son, Ferdinand I.

The palace (open Wed–Mon 8.30am–7pm; admission fee) has 1,200 rooms, 1,790 windows, and 34 staircases. The architect Vanvitelli's masterpiece is the grand staircase of marble and inlaid coloured stone surmounted by a double elliptical vault. Hidden behind the rim of the lower vault, musicians played to greet the king and his guests. At the top of the stairs Vanvitelli created a theatrical octagonal vestibule of columns, cupolas and arches. To one side, the gorgeous Palatine Chapel gleams in gold, green and white. Scarred antique columns along the sides are from the Serapeum of Pozzuoli. To the rear of the second courtyard is another Vanvitelli gem, the Court Theatre.

The magnificent park (open 8.30am–1hr before sunset) is worth visiting to see the Cascata Grande, an immense waterfall tumbling down a wooded hill. Shuttle buses run regularly between the palace and the Fountain of Diana at the foot of the 76-m (249-ft) Cascade.

Younger was made from this vantage point. Drive up to the Capo Miseno lighthouse at the top of the headland for one of the best views around.

Cuma

The holy of holies of the Phlegraean Fields was at Cuma, about 9km (5½ miles) from Bacoli, past a sandy bathing beach, the Marina di Fusaro, and Torregaveta, the end of the line on the Cumana railway. Founded by Greek colonists in the 8th century BC, Cuma became an important

The tunnel leading to the Sybil's Cave at Cuma

city that controlled the Phlegraean Fields region for nearly 500 years, until its decline under the Romans. The **Acropoli di Cuma** (open daily 9am–1hr before sunset) is surrounded by farmland studded with ruins, including an amphitheatre.

This is one of antiquity's most venerated sites: the famous **Cave of the Cumaean Sybil** (Antro della Sibilla), where the venerated prophetess answered questions about life and death and foretold the future. Although it never had the status of Delphi, people came from distant lands to consult the Sybil and receive her oracles. The cave is approached through a long keyhole-shaped tunnel lit by windows cut in the hillside.

From the Sybil's cave a Via Sacra paved by the Romans climbs to the ruins of a temple to Apollo and then further up to the site of a temple to Jupiter, later converted to a Christian church. The old Via Domiziana which runs back towards Pozzuoli passes under the **Arco Felice**, an arched defile 20m (65ft) high, cut into the rock by the Romans in the 1st century AD.

The view of Vesuvius across the bay from Naples

VESUVIUS

Seen from Naples, it is clear that the perfect cone of Vesuvius is actually a volcano within another, much larger volcano. The crater of the mother mountain, Monte Somma, rings Vesuvius to the left, its slope broken off in an eruption 17,000 years ago. The present 1,276-m (4,173-ft) cone has grown and changed shape through many eruptions, the most recent in the 1940s.

The 1944 explosion was preceded by earthquakes; then a stream of superheated lava roared down the Atrio del Cavallo, the valley between Vesuvius and Somma, travelling at 160kph (100mph). The road from Torre del Greco skirts this lava flow. It is surprising how quickly vegetation has covered the desolation – in spring the lower slopes are covered with golden broom. In winter the cone often gets a dusting of snow.

The road ends some 275m (900ft) below the volcano's rim. Then a half-hour walk up a steep path in the loose reddish cinders brings you to the top (ticket booth open 9am–2hrs before sunset; closed in bad weather). Good walking shoes are essential for this hike. Around the crater's edge, where wisps of steam drift from fumaroles, intrepid tourists pose for photos. Landslides have partially filled the inner cavity. The crater is 200m (654ft) deep and 600m (1,962ft) across. Views from up here across the bay are spectacular.

It is certain that Vesuvius will blow its top again one of these days, but it appears now to have entered a dormant cycle after erupting every few years since 1858. A 130-year period of inactivity preceded the calamitous eruption of 1631, when 3,000 people were killed, the mountain lost its top, and ashes fell as far away as Istanbul. There were also spectacular eruptions in 1872, 1906, 1929, 1933 and 1944.

POMPEII

In the 1st century AD, Pompeii was a prosperous commercial seaport at the mouth of the Sarno River. What happened to the 20,000 citizens in August AD79, was not as sudden as a bomb blast, but just as devastating. There had been warnings, and a bad earthquake 17 years earlier, although Vesuvius was green to its crest with vineyards and had never been considered threatening. Tremors shook the earth for several days in late August. Then around noon on 24 August a mushroom cloud shot up from the mountain and soon obscured the sun. Out of the darkness and growing stench of gas, a torrent of ashes, cinders and pumice pebbles fell on to the surrounding towns and settlements. The earth shuddered repeatedly and tidal waves rolled in from the sea. Worse was to follow as the mushroom cloud collapsed, raining a super-heated pyroclastic flow of rock, ash and dust down on the town, burning and suffocating the terrified citizens. When the sky cleared on 27 August Pompeii was buried under 7m

(23ft) of ash. This light material solidified with rain and time, preserving everything it encased in a time capsule.

Pompeii remained hidden until 1594, when workmen tunnelling for an aqueduct unearthed some walls and tablets. Serious excavations were begun in 1748, and most of the statues and valuables were removed in the next 150 years. Much of the treasure is in the Museo Archeologico Nazionale in Naples *(see page 36)*.

Around the Forum

Visits to the **Scavi di Pompeii** (excavations open Apr–Oct 8.30am–7.30pm, Nov–Mar 8.30am–5pm; last admission 90 min before closing; admission fee; ID is needed to hire the excellent audio headsets) begin at the Porta Marina, the sea gate, one of eight in the city walls. Actually there are two gates tunnelled here, one for pedestrians and one for the carts that brought loads up from the docks below onto the Via Marina. As with many of Pompeii's main thoroughfares, its lava paving stones are rutted by the passage of cart and chariot wheels.

The road leads past the Tempio di Venere (Temple of Venus) to the **Tempio di Apollo** (Temple of Apollo). The sundial on the pillar to the left of the raised temple is a reference to Apollo's role as god of the sun. Originals of the facing bronze statues of Apollo and his sister, Diana, goddess of the moon and the hunt, are in the Museo Archeologico Nazionale.

A few steps more and you are in the **Foro** (Forum), Pompeii's commercial and religious centre. At the head of the Forum stands the raised **Tempio di Giove** (Temple of Jupiter). To its right the central market, the **Macellum**, originally domed, is divided into stalls for produce vendors and *argentari*, moneychangers. Looming over all, straight ahead, is Vesuvius, far from dead and suddenly looking ominous.

When the disaster struck, many Pompeiians were overcome by poisonous fumes, their lives interrupted by the forces of nature. The wet ash solidified around their bodies like a mould that emptied in time as the flesh decomposed. By filling these 'moulds' with plaster, archaeologists have created lifelike casts of the victims. Several of these are to be seen in the **Horreum**, a sort of shed originally for storing and weighing grain stocked with wine jars and crockery, to the left of the Tempio di Giove. A man crouches, covering his face with his hands; a pregnant woman lies face down.

Across the Forum are several small temples, including one to Vespasian, the emperor who introduced public toilets (there is one at No. 28 on the west side). The buildings on the south end of the Forum served as the 'City Hall,' offices of the municipal council and other dignitaries.

After you see the Forum, there is no obvious itinerary to follow in Pompeii. The orderly Roman rectilinear layout of blocks and streets has been divided by archaeologists into

Pompeii street with a public drinking fountain

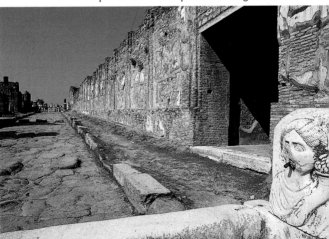

numbered Regions, Insulae (blocks) and houses, but the system is incomplete, changing, and can be confusing to the uninitiated. Start with the **Terme del Foro**, a small Roman bath just beyond the cafeteria and left on Via delle Terme. Note the delicate stucco work on the ceilings.

Passing through the Porta di Ercolano in the northwestern corner, the road descends along the romantic, tree-lined Via dei Sepolcri, flanked by ancient funerary monuments. At the lane's end, to the left, is the **Villa di Diomede** (Villa of Diomedes). The unusually big windows must have made this a sunny house, with pleasant views of the large garden. The body of the owner was found with the garden gate key in his hand and, beside him, a slave carrying a bag of valuables.

Dionysian mysteries are portrayed in the Villa dei Misteri

Revealing Villas

At this point you can leave the ruins proper, and follow signs to the **Villa dei Misteri** (Villa of the Mysteries). This elegant residence is decorated with the largest and most remarkable wall paintings surviving from Roman times. A sequence of scenes on a glowing red background follows the initiation of a newly married woman into the Dionysian mysteries, an orgiastic rite of Greek origin.

The most interesting houses are in the area northeast

of the Forum. Return to the crossroads above the Temple of Jupiter and follow Via della Fortuna. The second block on the left is entirely taken up by the **Casa del Fauno** (House of the Faun), a luxury villa with four dining rooms, one for each season, two peristyles and a small bath which made clever use of the heat produced by the oven in the adjacent kitchen. Most of the

The most prominent citizens of Pompeii were newly rich merchants who built showy houses (the Imperial court and Roman aristocrats had their holiday villas at fashionable Stabia, Herculaneum, Neapolis or near Baiae, across the bay). Most of Pompeii's population consisted of working people, artisans, shopkeepers and slaves.

house's treasures, including the mosaic of Alexander and the original dancing faun found in one of the two inner courtyards, are in the Archaeological Museum.

Another block along, in the Vicolo dei Vettii, is Pompeii's most famous house, the **Casa dei Vettii** (House of the Vettii). Carefully restored, it gives a good idea of how wealthy merchants lived. Paintings in the dining rooms and bedrooms show cupids engaged in typical activities of the town. Just inside the entrance is a fresco of Priapus, god of fertility, weighing his huge penis on a scale against a bag of gold. It used to be covered by a locked panel, and guards made a good income by giving visitors a peek. Now, in less prudish times, it's out in the open for all to see and giggle at. All over Pompeii you'll see phallic symbols on houses. These were to ward off the evil eye, similar to the red coral or plastic amulets worn today in southern Italy.

Brothels, Baths and Theatres

Follow the Vicolo dei Vettii back to the Via della Fortuna and cross to descend the Vico Storto. Note the large bakery

Bathtime

Visiting the baths was an important part of the Roman daily routine. First comes the vaulted changing room, lined with seats and niches for clothes. Off this are the *frigidarium*, for cooling off after the *tepidarium*, where a brazier heated the air, and the *caldarium*, with a pool and steam from an external boiler. Exercising was done in the adjoining gym, or *palaestra*, and there were separate facilities for women.

with mills on the left. Grain was poured in the top cylinder and the millstone turned by donkeys or slaves. Wind around to the left on Via degli Augustali to the Vicolo del Lupanare. Here, a series of small paintings illustrate the services offered in this rather cramped two-storey brothel, the **Lupanar Africani et Victoris**. Across the street, the doorway motto of the **House of Siricus** sums up Pompeii's parvenu creed: *Salve Lucru* ('Hail Money!').

Pompeii's largest baths, the **Terme Stabianae**, occupy nearly a block at the end of this street, with the entrance on the broad Via dell'Abbondanza. To the right of the portal is the men's section; beyond, in the women's baths, see the remains of the boiler room and the air space in the walls and floor where steam and hot air circulated.

Across the Via dell' Abbondanza to the right, follow the Via dei Teatri to the **Triangular Forum**, one of the city's earliest sacred precincts, to two theatres. A gateway leads into the forum, flanked by a long row of columns and shaded by old ilex and cypress trees. It's a quiet and restful spot, especially welcome on a hot day. At the rear, from the base of a 6th-century BC Doric temple, there's a good view across the Sarno River's clogged stream to modern Pompeii, Monte Faito and the Lattari range of the Sorrento peninsula.

The **Teatro Grande** could seat 5,000 people, and is still used today for concerts and other performances. The adjoining **Teatro Piccolo** or Odeion was originally roofed as a concert hall. A plaque reminded theatregoers that 'Claudio C.F. Marcello, Patrono' helped pay for the theatre. Most of Pompeii's public buildings were erected at the expense of rich citizens, who were often vote-seeking politicians. Beyond the large theatre is a colonnaded exercise field and the **Casa dei Gladiatori** (House of the Gladiators). Sixty-four bodies were found inside, some in chains, along with a rich store of weapons and armour, now housed in the Museo Archeologico Nazionale.

Commercial Pompeii

Returning by the Via Stabiana to the Via dell'Abbondanza, turn right and follow it into the area of the **Nuovi Scavi**, the 'new' excavations begun in 1911. This is a district of small industries, shops, taverns, hotels and the villas of a few wealthy businessmen. An effort has been made to reconstruct these premises and to leave some of their contents in place, including casts of bodies found here. Most Pompeian houses were two-storeyed, but the upper floors were crushed by the weight of ash. Here, many have been restored. Look for fine mosaic floors, stucco and painted wall decorations, and the trappings of artisans and

Pompeii's small theatre, or Odeion, was originally covered

A victim of the eruption

shopkeepers. Much of the graffiti is protected by glass along the street.

In a laundry, the **Fullonica Stephani** at No. 7 on the south side of Insula VI, vats for washing, dyeing and bleaching occupy the rear. A press stands to the left of the entry, where clothes were handed in through a window in the door. The upper floor held lodgings. Across the way, note the depth of ash-filled buildings still unexcavated. Around the corner to the right on this block are the House of the Underground Portico, where many bodies were found in the wine cellar; and the elegant **Casa di Menandro** (House of Menander). A collection of exquisite silverware, now in the Naples museum, was unearthed here. In the rear there's a chariot and the skeleton of a horse.

On the north side of the Via dell'Abbondanza, the **Thermopolium** of Asellina is a very well-preserved bar. Note graffiti advertising the names and attractions of prostitutes available in the upstairs cribs. At the end of the street, the **Villa di Giulia Felice** (Villa of Julia Felix) takes up most of the block. It was apparently a hotel, for there are 'rooms to let' signs on the walls. It had its own baths, a garden and shops.

Behind the villa is the **Anfiteatro** (Amphitheatre), the oldest surviving in Italy. Seating just 20,000, it was small by Italian standards. To the west, the nearby **Grande Palestra** is a vast exercise field 100m square, enclosed on three sides by a covered portico and pine and plane trees. Roots of the original trees were found, and the planting has been recreated.

Pompeii may be reached by the autostrada in 20 minutes, once you get outside Naples. There are frequent trains to the ruins from the Central Station at Piazza Garibaldi (on the Circumvesuviana line). Your hotel or the tourist information office can advise you on where to sign up for a guided tour.

HERCULANEUM

Just 12km (8 miles) southeast of the centre of Naples, Herculaneum (named after its legendary founder Hercules) is delightfully void of the crowds that inundate Pompeii. With just 5,000 inhabitants, the ancient town of Herculaneum was a smaller, more refined place than its bigger, brasher neighbour. While Pompeii was crushed under falling volcanic debris and red-hot cinders, Herculaneum was filled from the bottom up by ash and pumice carried on a torrent of ground-hugging superheated gas. Roofs did not cave in. The city was simply in-

Roman Remains

Until 1980 only a few bodies had been found in the ruins of Herculaneum, and it was believed that the estimated 5,000 inhabitants had managed to flee to safety. In 1980 came the discovery of hundreds of skeletons of men, women and children who had taken shelter in vaults at the marina. These skeletons provided a rare opportunity to study the size and health of typical individuals, for Romans cremated their dead and cemeteries contain only urns with ashes. Men were on average 1.65m (5ft 7 ins) tall, while women were considerably shorter. Teeth cavities were uncommon, perhaps because Romans did not have refined sugar in their diets.

Romans enjoyed a level of health care not available again until relatively modern times. A kit of instruments found in the House of the Surgeon in Pompeii included scalpels, forceps, catheters, implements for brain and eye surgery, suction cups, scissors, pincers and clamps.

undated by a flood that covered it to an average depth of 20m (65ft). This semi-liquid muck cooled and hardened to encase and protect balconies, furniture, food on the tables, and even glass window panes and wax writing tablets. Once discovered, the soft tufa sandstone was relatively easy to carve out.

Exploring Herculaneum

It's a 10-minute walk downhill from Ercolano station (a couple of stops from Pompeii on the Circumvesuviana line), through the soulless modern town to the excavation site of **Herculaneum** (open Apr–Oct 8.30am–7.30pm; Nov–Mar 8.30am–5pm; last admission 90 min before closing; admission fee). The city is laid out in the typical Roman grid pattern, with intersecting streets known as Decumani and Cardi. Beginning at Cardo III, on the left is the large **Casa d'Argo** (House of Argus), with Egyptian-looking columns. On past the intersection of the Decumanus Inferior are the **Terme del Foro** (Forum Baths), with women's and men's sections built around an exercise court. A Neptune whose legs turn into sea serpents decorates the mosaic floor of the tepidarium. Sea creatures painted on the ceiling over the cold plunge were reflected in its water.

The Palaestra of Herculaneum

East on the decumanus at the corner of Cardo IV is the much-photographed **Casa Sannitica** (Samnite House). The Samnites preceded the Romans here, as in Pompeii, and the house is a dignified structure of the 2nd century BC, one of the oldest in Herculaneum. Across the intersection, the overhanging roof, beams and door frame of the **Casa del Tramezzo del Legno** (House of the Wooden Partition) are original. Inside, note the cleverly hinged doors that slide on bronze grooves

An unusual water spout at a public fountain

to close off the atrium. A perfectly preserved wooden bed stands in the corner of an adjoining bedroom. A loaf of bread with a bite taken out of it was found in the dining room off the garden where lunch was being served as the disaster struck.

On the east side of Cardo IV above the Samnite House are the Weaver's House, the House of the Charred Furniture, the House of the Neptune Mosaic and the House of the Beautiful Courtyard, all remarkably preserved, with homely bits of everyday belongings, finely fashioned furniture, mosaics and frescoes. This road ends at a broad pedestrian street called the Decumanus Maximus and the edge of the still unexcavated Forum under the modern town. The **Palaestra of Herculaneum**, which extends under the path from the ticket booth, is only partly uncovered. In the centre a cross-shaped pool was fed by water from a bronze serpent coiled around a tree. Apparently games were in progress on the day of the eruption; stone 'shot-put' balls were found in the Palaestra.

The finest houses, at the end of Cardo V, had a view over the sea towards Capri from the embankment overlooking Herculaneum's marina. The grandest is the **Casa dei Cervi** (House of the Deer), where a pair of delicate sculptures of stags attacked by dogs was found. Neighbours to the left occupied the **Casa dell'Atrio a Mosaico** (House of the Mosaic Atrium), with its black-and-white checkerboard pavement that rippled under the shock of the eruption. This house had glassed-in porticos and a solarium looking out to sea.

Steps at the end of Cardo V descend to the small **Terme Suburbane** (Suburban Baths). Light filters into rooms through windows that once were glassed. The tubs, tanks, boilers, and even firewood for furnaces have been left as they were found. A frieze of warriors modelled in stucco decorates the dressing room above marble benches. Panelled wooden doors hang on their original hinges. A heavy marble basin lies on its side where it was tossed by the heaving earth. At the end of a corridor, graffiti in a room for private parties total up the bill for an order of cakes and record the pleasures of a homosexual encounter.

As you climb the steps to leave this small, elegant city, look behind you. The cone of brooding Vesuvius rises over the rooftops, only 7km (4½ miles) away. Beyond Herculaneum the road stretches around the bay to Torre Annunziata, where the glorious **Villa Poppaea** (open daily Apr–Oct 8.30am–7.30pm, Nov–Mar until 5pm, last entry 90 min before closing; admission charge; <www.pompeiisites.org>), built by the second wife of Emperor Nero, has some of the finest frescoes yet uncovered. It is a UNESCO World Heritage Site.

Buried treasures

The ruins of Herculaneum have yielded far more treasures of artistic value than Pompeii, although only a fraction of the city has been explored. Modern Ercolano sits directly on top of the site and half of the ancient town remains unexcavated.

A boat trip to beautiful Capri

CAPRI

The breathtaking beauty of Capri lives up to its legendary reputation. It is two sheer bluffs of rock joined in the middle by a lower, sloping saddle where white buildings cluster and spill down towards a busy, picturesque harbour.

This is the **Marina Grande**, where ferries laden with day-trippers come and go constantly amid much flinging of ropes and shouting on the dock. A small visitor's centre can be found at the end of the quay. You can take an open-top taxi or bus to the island's epicentre, the tiny Piazza Umberto I, better known as the **Piazzetta**. But the best way to reach Capri Town's main square is to take the funicular (departures every 15 minutes). The cable-car climbs the steep slope past lemon groves and flower-filled gardens, and delivers you to the terrace of Capri Town. The views from here are spectacular. To the left (west), Anacapri is perched on the massive grey limestone block of Monte Solaro, the island's highest point; to the right is Monte (or Salto di) Tiberio, the perch from which Tiberius ruled the Roman Empire. Below is the harbour and straight ahead across the bay are Vesuvius and the crags and cliffs of the Sorrentine peninsula.

Capri Town

If the terrace is Capri's balcony, the Piazzetta is its salon. The intimate little square is enclosed on three sides by cafés, bars and shops, and on the fourth by steps to the small 17th-century church of Santo Stefano. The Piazzetta is filled with umbrella-shaded tables and is most enjoyable in the evening when the day trippers have caught the last hydrofoil out and

Everyone's Favourite Island

Sooner or later, it seems, everyone comes to Capri. Augustus Caesar traded Ischia to the Neapolitans for it in 29BC. His successor, Tiberius, withdrew to Capri in AD26 when he was 67. He built the Villa Jovis and several other palaces and spent the last 11 years of his life on the island. During the Middle Ages Capri changed hands according to the chequered fortunes of Naples, and was repeatedly raided by pirates right into the late 1700s. The British occupied it from 1806 to 1808 during the Napoleonic Wars. The island finally came into its own with 19th-century Romanticism; after the Blue Grotto was 'discovered' in 1827 it became an obligatory stop on the Grand Tour. In 1906 Maxim Gorky created a school of revolution here and brought over Lenin as a director. In the next decades the success of Norman Douglas's *South Wind* and of *The Story of San Michele* by the Swedish doctor Axel Munthe spread the island's fame as a retreat of artists and eccentrics. Both the Germans and the Allies used it as a rest camp during World War II. After the war the international jet set moved in and, despite an increasing flood of tourists and day trippers, still claims Capri as its own.

the area is frequented by those fortunate enough to inhabit the island's myriad villas. There are no cars in the town proper – the lanes and alleys are far too narrow – but small electric tractors can get through to carry provisions to shops and hotels, as well as luggage. Taxis and buses stop some 50m (55yds) short of the Piazzetta, and a postage-stamp size visitor's centre at the base of the clock tower is available to answer any question in any language.

Santo Stefano overlooks Capri's heart, the Piazzetta

From the Piazzetta, take Via V. Emanuele, with its designer boutiques, past the legendary Hotel Quisisana and turn left to the **Certosa di San Giacomo** (open winter Tues–Sat 9am–2pm, Sun 9am–1pm; free), a 14th-century Carthusian monastery which houses a school and a museum of paintings from the 17th to the 19th centuries. The view from the monastery gardens encompasses the dramatic **Faraglioni** (a trio of rocks that rise 105m/345ft out of the sea) below and Monte Solaro above.

An equally breathtaking panorama can be seen from the terraced gardens of the nearby **Giardini di Augusto**, a little way along on Via Matteotti. Inside the shady gardens stands a memorial to Lenin, a curious intrusion into this playground of capitalism.

From the belvedere, you can see two higher lookout points – the **Punta del Cannone** and the **Castiglione** belvederes can both be reached along the Via Madre Serafina, which

Capri's coastline

starts behind the Santo Stefano church.

From the Parco Augusto, **Via Krupp** descends in dizzying corkscrew turns down to the **Marina Piccola**. The path is technically *chiuso* (closed) because of the danger of falling rocks, but this does not deter Capri regulars from using it. The Marina Piccola is their favourite bathing beach and watering hole. From the little strand you can rent a boat or kayak or join a cruise along the dramatic indented coast. Taxis linger here and buses run back up to town every 20 minutes.

Coastal Strolls

A very enjoyable walk, where you can enjoy a closer look at the Faraglioni, takes you from the Hotel Quisisana along the boutique-lined Via Camerelle to the **Punta Tragara**. If you're up to a modest hike of about an hour (along mostly shaded walkways), keep going along the coast path to the **Arco Naturale**. On the way you'll see the curious modern red house that the eminent Italian writer Curzio Malaparte had built in the late 1930s suspended over the sea. You'll pass a deep cave, the **Grotta di Matermania**, with some remains of a Roman sanctuary, and then climb steps up through pines to a natural limestone arch that frames a fine shot for photographers.

From the Piazzetta you can take either Via Longano or Via Le Botteghe to visit Tiberius's **Villa Jovis** (open daily 9am–1hr before sunset). It's a relatively hard 45-minute climb to the park at 335m (1,095ft). The villa was one of 12 Imperial palaces built on the island by Emperor Tiberius, who ruled the Roman Empire from Capri for 10 years.

Long ago looted of everything interesting, the site itself is not that exciting, but the **views** from here are breathtaking. The whole island is at your feet. Punta Campanella, on the tip of the Sorrento headland, is only 5km (3 miles) across the water. From this eagle's nest the reclusive, ageing Tiberius ruled the Western world and, according to Roman biographers, indulged in monstrous orgies. On the highest point is the infamous Salto di Tiberio (Tiberius' Leap), from where the sadistic emperor hurled his enemies and unsatisfactory lovers.

Anacapri

The island's only other town, Anacapri has none of the paparazzi's paradise nor beautiful-people glamour of Capri. At 283m (930ft) there's a quiet backwater charm in its meandering, tree-shaded streets, due to its relative remoteness. Noise and bustle are confined to the lane leading to Anacapri's tourist mecca, the tranquil, cool **Villa San Michele** (open May–Sept 9am–6pm; Apr and Oct 9.30am–5pm; Nov–Feb 10.30am–3.30pm; Mar 9.30am–4.30pm; admission fee). In stark contrast, the once peaceful path up to the villa has become a garish bazaar, selling local perfume and liqueurs, T-shirts, wind-up mandolins and the gamut of kitsch knick-knacks.

Nestled against the steep hillside, the Villa was built in 1896 on the site of an ancient Roman manor. It contains Axel Munthe's collection of Roman sculpture (both authentic and fake), antique furniture and prints. From the outside terraces there are breathtaking views of Monte Tiberio and the bay. There is almost always a throng milling around guides rattling off information in half a dozen languages.

Retracing your steps to the village square, you'll find the entrance to the chairlift (*seggiovia*) to **Monte Solaro**, at 589m (1,926ft) the highest point on the island. The chair rides over vineyards and pines to the peak and a 360-degree panorama of the island, Ischia, the Campanian coast, and the distant Appenine Mountains. A delightful trail through golden broom descends past the solitary and picturesque 14th-century Santa Maria Cetrella chapel on the lip of the precipice and back to Anacapri in 40 minutes.

Off the beaten track, down Via Orlandi to the Piazza San Nicola, is **San Michele Church** (open daily Apr–Oct 9am–7pm; Nov–Mar 9.30am–3pm) worth seeing for its beautiful floor, a naive Garden of Eden scene done in majolica tiles by an 18th-century artist.

The magical Blue Grotto

The Blue Grotto

From Anacapri the island's eastern side drops to low cliffs and coves reached by two roads, each served by a regular bus service. The bus marked 'Faro' goes to the lighthouse at Punta Carena, the island's wildest and least visited corner. This is a good swimming cove with a restaurant.

The other bus goes to a landing-stage next to Capri's most celebrated attraction, the **Grotta Azzurra** or **Blue Grotto** (open 9am–1hr before sunset) which you can also reach on organised tours, usually by boat from the Marina Grande.

When a wonder of the world becomes as famous as Capri's Blue Grotto, high expectations risk disappointment. Not so with this magical cavern and its glowing electric blue and silver waters: the Blue Grotto lives up to the rhapsodies it has inspired since it was 'discovered' in 1827.

The entrance to the Blue Grotto is an opening barely wide and high enough for a rowing boat, with passengers having to duck. Sunlight filtered from above through this opening irradiates the water with an ethereal blue that flashes and sparkles silver when a hand or oars are trailed below the surface. The best time for viewing is around midday. A flotilla of rowing boats constantly comes and goes through the tunnel to the accompaniment of shouts from boatmen and squeals of delight from tourists. The price of fame is overcrowding. It is unusual but not impossible to be one of a privileged few enjoying the grotto's beauty.

ISCHIA AND PROCIDA

Ischia is the largest and most diverse of the islands in the Bay of Naples, though a bus ride around its serpentine roads takes less than two hours passing through or near its six principal towns. It has a life of its own beyond tourism (though it swells to six times its population in summer months), mainly based on the production of a delightful light white wine (so famous in antiquity that Ischia was known to the Romans as Aenaria – wine-land), as well as a thriving fishing industry and the cultivation of chestnuts and lemons.

The volcanic island is a mass of green vines, orchards and pines, rising to the central peak of Monte Epomeo. Ischia's volcano is extinct, but it continues to steam away like a leaky boiler and underground activity is ubiquitous. As you travel around the island, you'll see puffs of white issuing from pipes in the back gardens of homes and cracks in the hillsides.

As well as yielding excellent wine, the volcanic terrain produces bubbling hot springs prized for their therapeutic powers since Roman times. Ischia boasts 70 hot springs and 100 thermal bath establishments. Italians and Germans who come here on a regular basis, swear by them for the effective treatment of rheumatism, arthritis, circulatory disorders, sciatica, even obesity and premature ageing. But you don't have to be suffering from an ailment to benefit. There's nothing more therapeutic for the weary traveller than a day spent wallowing in hot springs and thermal pools, maybe indulging in a mud bath, massage or facial treatment. There are scores of spa hotels around the island.

A Circular Tour of Ischia

In 1301 an eruption buried the principal town under a flow of lava that today is a pine grove and park separating **Ischia Porto** from the older town of **Ischia Ponte**, a 20-minute walk to the east. Ischia Porto is the main gateway to the island. To the right of the ferry dock an information office dispenses maps and booklets. Behind it is the parking space for buses that go round the island in both directions. If you want to do the driving yourself, the island is very easy to navigate and there are a number of car hire companies operating in the area (the tourist office will supply you with a list).

Ischia's most famous landmark, the **Castello Aragonese** (open Mar–Nov 9.30am–1hr before sunset; admission fee), caps a steep-sided fortified islet linked to Ischia Ponte by a causeway. The castle is privately owned, but you can visit the ruins and take an elevator to the top, where a small hotel occupies part of the former Convent of Poor Clares. On an adjoining terrace you'll find the entrance to the cemetery of the nuns. This is a chamber where the dead were seated against the walls and left to mummify. Further on are the cells where from 1851 to 1860 the Bourbon rulers of Naples imprisoned Italian nationalist patriots.

Continuing around the island clockwise: the road from Ponte climbs past vineyards and farms with storehouses carved out of the soft sandstone. From **Serrara Fontana**, it takes about an hour on foot to reach the closest point to the peak of **Monte Epomeo**, and not much less by the guided

A causeway connects Ischia Ponte to the Castello Aragonese

mules you can rent here. From the 760-m (2,500-ft) summit, another hour's hike will bring you down to towns on the other side of the island.

As the road descends abruptly, passing Serrara you get a good view towards Capri before the bus turns off at Panza for **Sant'Angelo**. This popular little seaside village has numerous restaurants around its promontory, La Roia, and the cafés and shops that make it a charming destination. Several hotels with thermal baths are perched on the mountainside just above the **Lido dei Maronti**, Ischia's longest and broadest volcanic black-sand beach. Steam hisses from fumaroles in the sand, and in nearby ravines are steamy caves and do-it-yourself mud baths used since antiquity.

The black volcanic sand of Ischia's Lido dei Maronti

As you approach **Forio**, you'll notice more and more signs in German. Since the 1980s, Ischia has been a favourite resort of German tourists, and Forio is their capital. The cafés on the village square and waterfront are lively international crossroads. Forio is also the centre of wine production, and wineries often invite visitors to sample their Epomeo vintages. The gleaming white church on the headland above the harbour is the **Santuario del Soccorso**. Inside it is filled with votive offerings for the protection of fishermen and sailors.

Just outside Forio is **La Mortella** (open Apr–Oct Tues, Thur, Sat, Sun, 9am–7pm; admission fee), the estate of English composer Sir William Walton (1902–83), famous for the gardens planted with over 1,000 exotic species. They were laid out by the landscape architect Russell Page and lovingly cultivated over 40 years by Walton's green-fingered widow, Lady Susana. After-

A tile dedicated to San Marco in the Santuario del Soccorso

noon concerts given by young musicians sponsored by the William Walton Trust are held at weekends.

At the island's western end is the picturesque cup-shaped harbour of **Lacco Ameno**. Every year on 17 May, the town explodes in an eruption of fireworks to celebrate the island's patron saint, Santa Restituta. Lacco Ameno's elegant spas make the unique boast of offering the most radioactive water and mud treatments in Italy.

Next comes **Casamicciola Terme**, a long stretch of thermal pools and hotels along the coast. The alkaline Gurgitello spring spouts 68°C (154°F) water and steam in which devotees cook themselves in boxes with just their heads sticking out of the top. Henrik Ibsen, who worked on *Peer Gynt* here in 1867, wouldn't recognise the place. Casamicciola was completely rebuilt after an earthquake in 1883, which took 3,000 lives. The town straggles towards Porto d'Ischia, completing the circuit.

Procida

Procida is the smallest and least touristic of the island trio. That's not to say that tourism doesn't play an important role.

In the summer months, the island's population is doubled by daytrippers from the mainland. They bring good business to the shops, hotels and restaurants, but not at the expense of the fishing and farming communities, which are still integral to the island's economy. Fishing is in the Procidan blood, while the rich volcanic soil is ideal for the cultivation of vineyards and citrus groves (Procida's lemons are reputedly the tangiest in Italy). The island covers only 4 sq km (1½ sq miles) and you can easily walk round it in a day – or, as this itinerary suggests, walk round half of it, loll on a beach after lunch, then catch a bus back to the port.

Ferries and hydrofoils dock at **Marina Grande**, a colourful jumble of boats and sun-baked houses. As you come off the boat, turn left and meander along the harbour, past the restaurants, bars, fishmongers and shops to the **Chiesa Santa Maria della Pietà** (1760). With your back to the white church, take

The charming traditional fishing village of Corricella

Via Vittorio Emanuele and walk uphill past the tourist office to Piazza dei Martiri and the yellow clifftop church of **Santa Maria delle Grazie**. It's a short climb from here to the **Abbazia San Michele Arcangelo** (open 9.45am–12.45pm and 3–6pm; closed Sun afternoon). The whitewashed domes of the abbey church rise above Terra Murata, the ruins of a citadel built to defend the island from Saracen attack. The three-naved church features a wooden coffered ceiling decorated with fine gold and a central painting of the archangel Michael by Luca Giordano (1699).

On your way back down to Piazza dei Martiri, stop at the terrace of the abandoned Castello and admire views of the ruined citadel above and **Corricella** below. This enchanting fishing village can be reached via a flight of steps from the piazza. Corricella is the most traditional village on the island, a warren of pastel-painted houses built into a sheltered cove, inter-connected by arches and stone stairways giving it a distinct Moorish feel.

Another set of steps at the far end of Corricella takes you back up to the main road. Turn left into Via Scotti, which becomes Via Vittorio Emanuele. Turn left again into the much quieter Via Pizzaco, which commands lovely views across the bay to the abbey and Corricella.

At the second fork in the road, veer right into Via Mozzo and continue hugging the coast, enjoying views of Capo Miseno on the mainland, until you reach Via Solchiaro. Turn left then right into Via S. Schiano which leads to **Marina Chiaiolella**, a berth for yachts and small boats. From here you can see the **Isola di Vivara**, a tiny volcanic island joined to Procida by a footbridge. Once a hunting ground for the Bourbon kings, Vivara is now a nature reserve and bird sanctuary.

The stretch of sand on the western side of the marina is Procida's longest and most popular beach (strictly two beaches: **Ciracciello** and **Ciraccio**). Stake out a patch of sand and enjoy a swim and siesta. A bus runs back to the port from here.

SORRENTO AND ITS PENINSULA

Sorrento is the *grande dame* of Neapolitan resorts, but there's very little sightseeing to do here. The most agreeable pastimes are strolling along lanes where flowering vines spill over garden walls, or walking down shady paths by the cliff edge, stopping for refreshment at a terrace bar or café perched above the bay. These days the town is above all a base for exploring the Sorrentine peninsula, the islands and the Amalfi coast. Bus tours are what keeps this formerly elitist resort town in business, and tourism is still its game.

Hydrofoils and ferries from Naples or Capri dock at the **Marina Piccola** where jostling hotel porters and tour guides await. The winding road from the harbour leads to Sorrento's main square, the **Piazza Tasso** name after Sorrento's favourite son, the Renaissance poet Torquato Tasso (1544–95). If you arrive by car or by train, you'll reach the Piazza Tasso via the **Corso d'Italia**, Sorrento's central thoroughfare.

Sorrento's landmarks can be visited in short walks from this main square. The tourist office (also known as the Circolo dei Forestieri) on Via L. de Maio just off the square, will supply you with a map of the town. Heading west from the square, Corso Italia leads to the **Duomo,** Sorrento's cathedral. Although much altered over the centuries, it has noteworthy inlaid wood stalls in the choir with the *intarsia* work still carried on by Sorrentine craftsmen.

Cross the Corso and wander into the heart of the old centre of Sorrento; its street plan dates back to Greek and

Intarsia

Intarsia – detailed and delicate wood inlay – is the craft most associated with Sorrento, and numerous *intarsia* workshops can still be found in the upper part of the town. Once ubiquitous, the intricate and understandably expensive work now takes some tracking down.

Roman times. The skinny Via Cesareo is lined with souvenir shops selling bright ceramics, inlaid boxes and trinkets, bottles of *limoncello*, the sweet and sticky local liqueur, and a whole host of knick-knacks decorated or scented with lemons. On the corner of Via Giuliani is the **Sedile Dominova**, a 16th-century loggia that was the summer meeting place for Sorrentine aristocrats. Today, it is the domain of old men who sit around tables under the majolica dome playing cards and talking politics.

Palm trees grace Sorrento's main square, the Piazza Tasso

From here, pick your way through the narrow streets to Villa Comunale, a shady park at the cliff edge with wonderful views over the Bay of Naples. Sorrento's grand and formerly grand hotels (Tramontano, Excelsior, Bellevue, etc.) are ranged along the clifftop. At the edge of the park stands the baroque church of **San Francesco**, with its onion-dome belltower.

From the terrace of the park, you can take the steps or lift down to the beach platforms of **Marina Piccola**. Sorrento is not known for its beaches, but if your hotel is lacking a pool, you can come down to one of the handful of public *stabilimenti* and hire a parasol and sun lounger for a small fee.

The Via Veneto leads from the Villa Comunale to the Piazza Vittoria. From here, follow Via Marina Grande down through the old Greek gateway to the harbour. Confusingly

Sunbathing in Marina Piccola

called **Marina Grande**, the 'Big Port', it is in fact the smaller and more down at heel of the two, but is all the more charming for it. This is one of the most authentic corners of Sorrento and an ideal dinner location.

Returning to the Piazza Tasso, cross the ravine and follow the Via Correale east past parks and hotels to the **Museo Correale di Terranova** (open Wed–Mon 9am–2pm; admission fee), the only real point of cultural interest in town. The 18th-century villa (with lovely gardens) now houses a museum whose offerings include an excellent collection of 17th-century Neapolitan paintings, inlaid *intarsia* furniture and Capodimonte porcelain of the region.

Exploring the Peninsula

The road from Sorrento to the tip of the peninsula begins with the Corso as it leads out of town towards Massa Lubrense. Soon after leaving Sorrento, a turning to the right, marked by a sign, leads down a very narrow lane through fields and olive groves to the ruins of the Roman **Villa of Pollio Felix**, on a superb site at the tip of a small cape. Boatmen from Sorrento can take you to this pretty picnic spot, where there is good swimming off the rocks.

There is swimming, too, on the small stony beaches and coves out on the cape, some accessible only by the boats available for rent at fishing villages such as Marina di Puolo and Marina della Lobra, the little harbour below Massa Lubrense. It's a great area for snorkelling.

Termini is the departure point of one of the loveliest walks on the peninsula. Park outside the yellow church, stock up on water and a cake or snack from the bar, then follow the signs to **Punta Campanella**. The road soon gives way to a footpath which descends slowly through terraced lemon and olive groves, past a Saracen watchtower, to the tip of the peninsula. The views from here are breathtaking and Capri is so close you could almost reach out and touch it. The uphill return is more strenuous. Allow for about two hours in total.

Just beyond Termini, the road to Nerano winds down steeply to the popular **Marina del Cantone** beach on the Gulf of Salerno. Small hotels, *pensioni* and apartments in villages atop the peninsula's ridge are inexpensive bases for exploring the coast and enjoying the spectacular views on foot, by bus or by car.

The best panoramic view is from the medieval convent **Il Deserto** (open Apr–Sep 8.30am–12.30pm, 4–8pm; Oct–Mar 8.30am–12.30pm, 2.30–4.30pm; ring the bell if the gate is closed), on a terraced hill above the village of **Sant' Agata sui due Golfi** (396m/1,300ft above sea level and always favoured for its vistas). It takes in the whole region, from Capri to Ischia and Cape Miseno.

The road back to Sorrento from Sant'Agata is the 'Nastro Azzurro' (Blue Ribbon), the first stretch of the scenic route to Positano and the Amalfi coast.

The belvedere at Villa Cimbrone, Amalfi Coast

THE AMALFI COAST

One of the most beautiful excursions in the world, the fabled Amalfi coast drive consists of one astonishing view after another, but you won't see much of them if you are behind the wheel. The road is a veritable marvel of engineering – a narrow, serpentine ribbon cut out of the rock, clinging to the contours of mountains that drop steeply into the sea. Drivers worry about dropping into the sea, too, as they navigate curves with the mountain wall on one side, only a low barrier on the other, and huge tour buses bearing down ahead. Timid drivers should seriously consider travelling by private taxi or public transport. Parking is another nightmare.

Suspended between sea and sky for most of its 45km (28 miles), the drive links a string of cliff-hanging towns and coastal communities that were once the territory of Amalfi, the oldest maritime republic in Italy.

Positano

Coming from Sorrento, the first (and the coastline's most fashionable) stop is **Positano**, a jumble of pastel-hued, cube-shaped houses that spill in terraces down the flanks of a ravine under a ring of mountain cliffs. There's nothing close to level in Positano except the beach, the semi-sandy **Spiaggia Grande**. Instead of streets, the town has a network of steep steps. Fortunately, a bus (8am–midnight) makes a regular circuit from the Amalfi drive along Positano's only road and back, coming fairly close to most hotels and connecting Positano with neighbouring coastal towns. There are a few parking garages that offer only limited hope of available space.

The road does not penetrate the oldest part of Positano and the beach area, still only reachable on foot through a maze of whitewashed alleys. The principal one, **Via dei Mulini**, passes the inviting courtyard of the 18th-century **Palazzo Murat**, (now a gracious hotel; *see page 133)* where summer concerts are held. The pathway is lined with racks of resort fashions, the wares of sandal-makers and galleries of every description. Positano was once known for its casual resortwear, a look that outgrew its appeal some decades ago. It has discreetly up-market hotels, yachts riding just offshore, casual but good restaurants, and bougainvillaea-draped villas belonging to an international roster of the rich and famous. At the height of the summer season the grey sands of the Spiaggia Grande disappear under row upon row of reclining chairs and ranks of beached boats for hire, and it's hard to find a table on the arboured terraces of the popular seafront restaurants.

A lane along the cliff to the right (west) of the Spiaggia Grande (and the concrete **Marina Grande** pier there) winds past a round watchtower and leads to the **Fornillo Beach**, also commandeered by beach-chair renters. A number of idyllic uncrowded coves are nearby, reached by hiring a rowing boat or being taken out by a private service (see agency booths set up on shore for these short excursions). Boat trips further afield are popular, to fishing villages up and down the coast and out to the three private isles **I Galli**, once owned by the ballet star Rudolf Nureyev and now in the hands of a European corsortium.

After Positano the drive reaches **Praiano**, a village scattered along the Capo Sottile headland. Less sophisticated (and less crowded) than Positano, it nevertheless accommodates some of Positano's overflow. At the round Saracen defence tower, steps go down to Marina di Praia's beach, where boats can be hired.

It is impossible to compare the views along this coast – each more magnificent than the next. Ancient footpaths wind down to small secluded coves where you can swim off the rocks. The next headland is **Conca dei Marini** ('Seafarers' Basin'), with a large parking space for the lift down to the **Grotta Smer-**

The majolica dome of San Luca Evangelista church, Praiano

alda, the Emerald Grotto. This large illuminated cavern's water is a brilliant gem-like green and is a popular sight. A landslide breached the cave, letting in the sea and covering stalagmites and stalagtites (Capri's contending Blue Grotto has none of these) reflected in the emerald depths. But the hassle of high-season crowds and climbing in and out of boats may discourage those other than dedicated grotto fanciers.

Amalfi

As the road approaches **Amalfi**, 18km (11 miles) southeast of Positano, and descends towards the shore, it passes beneath tiny terraces cut into the cliffs where lemons, olives and vines are grown in soil laboriously carried up in baskets over the centuries. After a tunnel, Amalfi appears – all white houses with red tile roofs, joined together in what seems a single construction. The buses that line the seafront promenade testify that tourism is the main industry, but in its 11th- and 12th-century heyday Amalfi rivalled Pisa and Genoa as a mighty maritime power in the Mediterranean (and Italy's first), when its population swelled to more than 100,000.

Nowhere is Amalfi's architecture more visibly influenced by its maritime dealings with the Arab world and points East than in its showpiece **Duomo di Sant'Andrea** (open Apr–June daily 9am–7pm; July–Sep 9am–9pm; Oct and Mar 9.30am–5pm; Nov–Feb 10am–1pm and 2–4.30pm). It is Amalfi's focal point, sitting atop a monumental 62-step staircase that confirmed the town's importance. Remodelled several times – principally in the 13th century – since its 9th-century founding, the cathedral dedicated to St Andrew retains its Moorish-Arabesque character. Its small cloister, the evocative location of summer concerts, is one of southern Italy's loveliest.

The compact town is divided between the **Piazza del Duomo** and the store-lined Via Genova, and the bustling waterfront **Piazza Flavio Gioia** (named for the Amalfi-born

Amalfi's spectacular setting has long attracted artistic travellers

inventor of the compass), made up of a bus and car park and the pier where boats depart for the islands, Naples and Positano. Meander around town and you'll stumble upon the narrowest possible staircase alleys, or *salitas*, that climb the hills on either side. Exploring these byways can lead to picturesque corners. One, above the Duomo's Cloister of Paradise, leads to the tiny 10th-century **Santa Maria Maggiore**, snuggled into the almost seamless construction of Amalfi houses and *salitas*.

Continuing 15 or 20 minutes up the main Via Genova you can soon hear the river gurgling underfoot. It emerges where the outskirts of Amalfi become the **Valle dei Mulini**, Valley of the Mills. Now in ruins, these were the first paper mills in Europe. The Amalfitani learned the process from the Arabs, who had picked it up from the Chinese. Handmade paper from the Amatruda paper mill, the only one still functioning, is sold in Amalfi in the small gift shops near the Duomo.

Ravello

The road from Atrani, just past Amalfi, twists up the dark, narrow Dragone Gorge to **Ravello**, a medieval relic pinned to a ridge 362m (1,184ft) above the sea. Of all the coast's spectacular views, Ravello's is considered by many to be the best. Seductive views are a modern notion, however; the merchant/founders of Ravello chose the site because it is naturally protected by cliffs on three sides and was easy to defend against raiders.

Most of Ravello's lanes are too narrow for vehicles (so drivers must leave their cars outside town), but perfect for leisurely rambles. The main square is dominated by the austere 11th-century **Duomo** (open daily 8.30am–1pm, 3–8pm), the cathedral dedicated to patron saint San Pantaleone (his feast day is celebrated on 27 July) and founded in 1086.

Just beyond the piazza, in the much photographed **Villa Rufolo** public gardens (open daily 9am–sunset), huge old pines and cypresses shade the shattered walls and towers of the 11th-century Rufolo castle. Concerts of classical music are held in warm weather months on the beautiful flowering terrace suspended above the sea. This is the inspirational spot of which Wagner wrote in 1880, 'This is Klingsor's garden,' the embodiment of his vision for the third act of *Parsifal*.

A short walk from the monastery leads to Ravello's other enchanting gardens, the **Villa Cimbrone** (open daily 9am–sunset). This dramatic residence (now operating as a hotel; *see page 134*) and garden is the caprice of a 19th-century English owner who created it out of medieval bits and pieces. The romantic atmosphere is not lessened by a plaque (put up after her death) recording that the 'divine Greta Garbo' stole 'hours of secret happiness' here with Leopold Stokowski in the spring of 1938. At the end of an alley of trees and flowering shrubs is a bust-lined clifftop belvedere on the very tip of Ravello's ridge whose view over the entire Bay of Salerno, wrote local resident author Gore Vidal, was 'the most beautiful in the world' – certainly worth the detour from the coast below.

A scenic road from Ravello winds over the mountains to join the Naples–Salerno *autostrada* at Nocera. This alternative route makes it easy to visit Pompeii in a day trip from the coast resorts.

PAESTUM

Three of the finest Greek temples in existence have survived remarkably intact for more than 2,500 years on an isolated coastal plain south of Salerno. Greek colonists founded Poseidonia (named after the sea-god Poseidon) in the 6th century BC. The Romans renamed it Paestum in 273BC when they took over the settlement and enlarged it. After the fall of Rome, the city sank into a decline, and more or less vanished from the map and history until the 18th century, when Charles III, the indefatigable Bourbon builder, had a road constructed across the plain. Cutting through the underbrush, the labourers uncovered ruins and ran the road right across them, much as you find it today.

The most direct route from Naples to Paestum is the A3 *autostrada* for 73km (44 miles), exiting at Battipaglia and continuing another 20km (12½ miles) on well-marked roads through farmland to the ruins.

The entrance to **Paestum** (open daily 9am–1hr before sunset) is near the southern end. Straight ahead of the entrance in a grassy field are Paestum's greatest temples, the **Temple of Poseidon** (or Neptune) and, to its left, the

Unique antiques

The Paestum museum (which closes an hour before the ruins) has a collection of terracotta pots, fragments of Doric friezes and tomb murals – the only ancient Greek paintings to survive anywhere.

The Temple of Ceres at Paestum dates from c.500BC

Basilica – both names having been incorrectly applied in the 18th century. It was later proved that both temples were dedicated to Hera, wife of Zeus.

The Basilica is Paestum's earliest construction, guessed to be around 565BC, pre-dating the Parthenon of Athens by nearly a century. Its somewhat heavy and bulging fluted columns and the flattened discs of the Doric capitals mark it as archaic, when the Doric style was evolving. The Temple of Poseidon was built about 100 years later on the pattern of the Temple of Zeus at Olympia, its 36 fluted Doric columns making it one of Magna Graecia's finest.

Behind these temples a paved Roman road runs alongside an area on the right that held the city's principal public buildings and passes the third temple. This dignified structure, known as the **Temple of Ceres**, was raised between the time of the Basilica and the Temple of Poseidon and was actually dedicated to Athena.

WHAT TO DO

SPORTS

There are sports facilities in Naples and throughout the coastal resort region, both for those who like to participate and for spectators. If you want to play **tennis**, the courts of the Tennis Club Napoli are in the Villa Comunale at the Piazza della Vittoria end and on the Vomero on Via Rossini; have your hotel call to book a court, especially in resort towns. If you prefer **golf**, there's a nine-hole golf course in Pozzuoli, just outside of Naples. **Fitness clubs** and **gyms** are listed in the yellow pages under *Impianti sportivi e palestre*.

You have to go well beyond the Naples harbour to find safe **swimming**. The water is clean around Cape Miseno, where numerous bathing beaches can be reached by the Cumana rail line. Far more enticing are the beaches of the islands, Sorrentine peninsula and Amalfi coastline. Capri and Ischia are stony shingle; swimming in general is done off the rocks. The same is true for Sorrento's bathing platforms beneath the cliff, while visitors to Amalfi and elsewhere often ferret out idyllic little coves. **Snorkelling** equipment is available for rent on Positano's beach (relatively large, considering the area), and there's **windsurfing** and **sailing** at many resorts.

The Mediterranean is overfished, but it's still possible to go **fishing** for tuna and swordfish in boats from the small ports of the Sorrento peninsula. A line and a rod are all you need to join those angling from the rocks beyond Naples' Santa Lucia, but remember the waters here are hardly pristine.

For **hiking**, there are lovely walks in the hills on Sorrento's cape, in the Monti Lattari backing the Amalfi coast and

Seaside fun on Capri

There is no shortage of hills and mountains to climb

around the Phlegraean Fields, as well as gentle climbs up Monte Epomeo on Ischia and Monte Faito from Castellamare di Stabia.

Horse racing is a year-round spectacle at the Ippodromo di Agnano only a few kilometers from the stadium off the *tangenziale*.

The Napoli **football** club, one of the most historic in Italy, was recently promoted to Serie A after years in the financial and playing doldrums; the club remains hard to beat for the exuberant enthusiasm of its many fans. The 78,000-seat San Paolo stadium in Fuorigrotta hosted World Cup games in 1990.

SHOPPING

Shops are open in Naples from 9am (the more stylish the shop, the later it opens) to around 1pm and from 3.30 or 4pm until 7.30 or 8pm. During the summer season, shops in resort towns close only when the last tourists leave the streets.

Look for **antiques** off the Piazza della Vittoria, in the Vias Arcoleo and Gaetani, behind the Riviera di Chiaia, and in Via Santa Maria di Constantinopoli near the National Museum. Old chests, mirrors, engravings, porcelain and candlesticks might have come from a palazzo. Browse around the weekend open-air flea market in the Villa Comunale for junk and gems.

High fashion and famous labels are found around Piazza dei Martiri and Via Chiaia. Shoes, a much-admired Italian product, are also offered on the Via Toledo, some made in the cottage-industry factories in the back streets of Naples. In Capri, Ischia, Positano and Sorrento, there are innumerable shops and stalls selling summer fashions, as well as handicrafts – sandals, belts, straw hats and inexpensive handmade jewellery. There's a vast open-air second-hand clothes market at Resina, adjoining Herculaneum. You'll find first-rate garments at knock-down prices in a typically Neapolitan setting.

Ceramics of all kinds, whether shapes copied from Greek and Roman urns, jugs and plates, or typical patterns of animals, fish and lemons, are the speciality of Vietri sul Mare and can be found All along the Amalfi coast. Other forms are made and sold at Paestum.

The **figurines** of handpainted terracotta made in Naples for Christmas cribs – called *presepi* – are an art handed down over the generations of families living around the Via San Gregorio Armeno in the Spaccanapoli quarter of the old city. Here, too, there's a great difference in quality from plastic moulded run-of-the-mill shepherds and *pulcinella* figures to the justifiably expensive individual set pieces. Even if you don't buy anything, these chock-a-block shops are definitely worth visiting.

Cameos and **carved coral** are worked while you watch in the factory salesrooms of

Classic cameos

Cameos have been a Neapolitan art form since Roman times. In antiquity, white glass layered onto blue was carved to stand out in relief. Since the 19th century, seashells have replaced glass. Carvers scrape away the outer part of the shell to expose the white layer. The cameo design is painstakingly carved from the white material, often under a magnifying glass, leaving a background of chestnut-hued shell.

Coral jewellery in a Capri shop

Torre del Greco, 13km (8 miles) from Naples, on the way to Vesuvius and Pompeii. Most tours to the historical sites include a stop at a cameo factory. These traditional ornaments are sold wherever foreigners are likely to congregate, but there's more variety and opportunity to shop around here where they are made. Ask a shopkeeper to show you with a magnifying glass how to tell fine cameo carving from ordinary products.

Intarsia is the inlaid wood of different types and colors, which is made into boxes, trays, tables, frames and many other forms in Sorrento. This, too, can be found elsewhere, but it's more fun seeing the delicate process carried out in a workshop and learning from the experts how to distinguish fine inlays from dyed and engraved designs.

Italian **housewares** are often very handsomely designed. You can find such things on the Via Toledo in Naples. You might want to take back a 'Napoletana' pot for making *espresso* on your stove, or even an electric steam *espresso* machine.

Comestibles of various kinds make good gifts. In Capri and Sorrento you can find bottles of lemon and basil liqueurs. The **wines** of Ischia and Ravello are interesting. Good *vergine* olive oil, sun-dried tomatoes, a string of small bright red peppers, or a rope of garlic might jazz up your kitchen.

Records, **cassettes** and **CDs** of old Neapolitan folksongs are sold in street markets, but you might want to try Verdi's publishers, the house of Ricordi in the Galleria in Naples.

ENTERTAINMENT

The greatest show in Naples, apart from the city itself, is surely opera in the Teatro San Carlo. Even if you are not fanatical about opera, don't miss the chance to see a performance in this landmark temple of *bel canto*; the hall itself is a gem. The season runs all year except August (box office open Tues–Sun in winter; Mon–Fri in summer; tel: 081-7972331; <www.teatrosancarlo.it>).

Concerts, from classical to rock, are part of the summer programmes of all the resort towns, and each resort has its own information office for details. To find out what's happening in Naples, ask for *Qui Napoli*, the free monthly bulletin (with foreign translations of key information) distributed through most hotels and tourist offices. The Italian radio's Alessandro Scarlatti Orchestra presents a series of concerts in the Capodimonte Park in July. During the summer, evening concerts and ballet are performed in the outdoor theatres of Pompeii, and in the 'Vesuvian Villas', restored palaces near Portici along the bay.

Once upon a time country folk may have danced the **tarantella**, slapping tambourines and snapping their fingers. Today this type of folklore exists only as an activity staged by tourist outfits and bears no relationship to anything in real life. The spirit of Naples and its surrounding communities is better evoked at the **street festivals** held in every district for a saint's day or other remembrance *(see facing page)*. Many are in mid-summer, often involving fireworks and orgies of eating that are enjoyed by holidaymakers too.

NIGHTLIFE

In the evenings, young people crowd squares in their neighbourhoods, lingering outside pizzerias and bar/caffès, lounging by their motor scooters, courting in the shadows. Naples nightlife is not exactly hectic. What Neapolitans most like to do in the evening is go to a cinema or theatre, then on to a restaurant – in summer preferably one outdoors near the water or up on a hill with a view – where they have a long-drawn-out meal with friends and relatives, drink wine and listen to music. This isn't a bad recipe for the tourist, either. If you're lucky you may hear *O Marinariello* and *Santa Lucia* sung to a mandolin, with a full moon sparkling on the bay.

There are nightclubs, late-night bars and discos on the bay, including Chez Moi (Via Parco Margherita 13), which attracts an older crowd. Arenile (Via Cordoglio 14, Bagnoli) is slightly more hip, while Otto (Salita Cariati 32) is the place for jazz and blues. Every village has its square, and every resort has its central hub, where the pleasures of golden days are transmuted into silvery nights. Maybe it's all that fresh air, sunshine and exercise, but bedtime comes earlier by the sea. Those who do see the wee hours usually spend them in conversation at an open-air bar or caffè.

Easter processions are held throughout the region

Calendar of Festivals

6 January *Naples* Epiphany: an old witch known as La Befana distributes presents to children on the Piazza del Plebiscito.

February *Carnevale* The beginning of Lent is celebrated with parades. Children dress in carnival costumes; lasagne is the carnival dish.

19 March *Naples* Festa di San Giuseppe: special cakes known as *zeppole* are traditionally eaten.

Easter Good Friday processions all over the region, especially on Procida and in Sorrento and Massa Lubrense. The Monday after Easter, frenetic dancing known as 'Ndrezzata ('intertwined') takes place at Buonopane on Ischia. Dancers wear traditional costumes and carry rolling pins.

May (first weekend) *Naples* Phials of San Gennaro's blood and his head in a silver reliquary are carried in procession from the Duomo to Santa Chiara, where the blood supposedly liquefies.

14 May *Capri* A statue of the town's patron saint, San Constanzo, is carried in procession to the sea, where participants are blessed.

15 May *Positano* Feast of the patron saint, San Vito.

24 June *Ischia* Festival of San Giovanni Battista. More frantic 'Ndrezzata dancing (see Easter Monday, above).

27 June *Amalfi* Festival of Sant'Andrea: costumes, fireworks, music and the blessing of the fishing fleet.

26 July *Ischia* The patron saint, Sant'Anna, is honoured with a torchlight procession of hundreds of boats.

27 July *Ravello* Feast of San Pantaleone celebrated with a spectacular firework display.

15 August *Ferragosto* The Assumption is celebrated all over the region. Positano has a procession followed by fireworks.

17 September *Naples* Feast of San Gennaro: the faithful gather in the Duomo to witness the liquefication of the saint's blood.

Christmas *Naples* Churches compete to build the finest *presepe* (nativity scene). Concerts held in city churches.

31 December *Naples* New Year is ushered in with a concert and fireworks in the Piazza del Plebiscito.

EATING OUT

At its best, the food of southern Italy is essentially inspired home cooking, based on what's best that day in the market. You'll see housewives critically making their choices in the street markets of Old Naples – perfect plum tomatoes for sauce, big bunches of basil and flat-leaf parsley, fennel, artichokes, fat aubergines (eggplants), fresh-picked chard, *bettola* greens, golden peppers, and hot, red *peperoncini*. There are also big onions and strings of garlic, of course, lemons with their leaves on to prove freshness, and virgin olive oil. The greatest treats, now quite expensive, are fish and other seafood.

The cosmopolitan tide that floods the resorts of the coast has brought all sorts of non-Neapolitan dishes to the menus of hotels and restaurants. There are elegant restaurants in

Local produce at the market

Santa Lucia and Pizzofalcone, and more along the coast (*see Recommended Restaurants on page 135*). But often a simple *trattoria*, with paper tablecloths and mamma at the stove, serves the most typical and satisfying fare. Dining *alfresco* in the shade of a vine arbour, or on a quay where fishing boats rock on the tide, or beside a wood-fired pizza oven that brings forth a sizzling *pizza margherita*, can be the high point of your day.

PASTA

Pasta is served as a first course, with meat or fish to follow. Eating pasta as often as twice a day, day after day, is considered essential to human well-being, and it's a notion that's difficult to contest.

Anything cooked *alla napoletana* will be bathed in a full-flavoured tomato *(pomodoro)* sauce. Made simply with lightly cooked fresh tomatoes, it has no peer. This blissful union of ingredients was some time coming, because, although pasta had been around since Roman times (a half-eaten plate of *pasta e fagioli*, which is still served locally today, was found in the ruins of Pompeii), the Neapolitans had to wait until the Spanish brought tomatoes back from Mexico in the 16th century before the recipe was complete.

Oil and garlic with parsley *(aglio e olio)*, clam sauce *(alle vongole)*, or *alla siciliana*, with chilli peppers, are other favourites. Besides spaghetti (from *spago*, meaning string), there are dozens of pasta shapes made in factories around Naples from firm durum wheat. *Rigatoni* and *ziti* are thick tubes, *farfalle* resemble butterflies, and *conchiglie* are shell-shaped. *Tagliolini* are very thin strands. *Fettuccine* are flat and often made with egg in the dough. *Tagliatelle* are from the same dough and flat, but cut as thin as spaghetti, while *lasagne* are very broad and are usually baked with their sauce.

The most popular type of pasta is *pasta asciutta*, made from a simple flour and water dough then dried. This is normally factory produced, whereas *pasta fresca*, includes eggs for a softer dough and is made at home. Most restaurants usually carry one or two of the latter, changing daily.

PIZZA

The pizza of Naples has conquered the world, though the limp, soggy stuff often dished up abroad as fast food bears little resemblance to the real thing. Since the early 19th century Neapolitan pizzerias have been relaxed and friendly places where people can eat simply and cheaply. The secret of 'real' pizza is in the brick oven and the high temperature that makes the dough puffed and crunchy round the edges. (That is why pizza is usually served only in the evening: not many eateries can crank up their ovens to maximum heat by lunchtime.)

The *margherita* is the perfect form of pizza, named after Queen Margherita, who in 1889 wanted to try the food of the people, and chose this simple version as her favourite. Allegedly, she was patriotically attracted by the tomatoes, mozzarella cheese, oregano and basil of its topping, reflecting the red, white and green of the Italian flag. Other authentic Neapolitan pizzas include *napoletana*, made with tomatoes, mozzarella, and anchovies; *marinara*, a simple combination of fresh tomatoes and juicy new-season's garlic; and *quattro stagioni*, the famous Four Seasons, divided into quarters with anchovy strips, then piled high with a variety of toppings.

Italian staple

When southern Italian families moved to the industrialised north in search of work in the 1950s and 1960s, they took their favourite food with them. Today, an estimated 7 million pizzas are made and sold in Italy every day.

Pizza fresh from the oven

REGIONAL SPECIALITIES

At a typical restaurant the waiter will point out the day's specials. Usually they will be the best bargain. Look around and see what others are eating.

Starters might include *crostini*, toasted rounds of bread topped with tomato, mozzarella and anchovy, sometimes with chicken livers. Baked peppers are stuffed with chopped olives, capers and anchovies (*peperoni ripieni*), or roasted and peeled, then simply bathed in light olive oil and topped with anchovies. *Mozzarella in carrozza* is sliced cheese sandwiched in bread, then dipped in beaten egg and lightly fried. For a lighter start to the meal choose *insalata caprese*, a tomato, mozzarella and fresh basil salad from Capri. Deep-fried squid (*calamaretti*) and whitebait (*cecenielli*) make tasty starters. And there's always salami and the northern standby, thinly sliced Parma ham (*prosciutto*) with melon or fresh figs (*fichi*).

Fish on ice at the market

Seafood is popular throughout the region. Naples is renowned for its *fritto misto di mare*, a huge pile of mixed fish deep-fried in a light and crispy batter. Lobster *(aragosta)* or big grilled prawns *(gamberi)* can be your reward after a hard day's sunbathing. *Zuppa di pesce*, a hearty fish soup, a delicious assortment of seafood cooked with tomatoes, garlic and spices, makes a meal in itself. *Triglie*, little red mullet, are good fried, while *spigola* (sea bass) is excellent grilled. The best restaurants will present the fish for your approval before cooking it and will charge according to the weight. Fresh fish can be expensive: confirm the price to avoid surprises when the bill comes.

Main courses are often simple, flavoursome stews and roasts, such as *coniglio all'ischitana*, an Ischian speciality of rabbit stewed in the local white wine with tomatoes and rosemary, or *spezzatino*, a veal stew with vegetables. More elaborate, Sicilian-influenced dishes may also be available – a remnant of Naples' royal past. Beef steaks are not the best choice in the South but pork *(maiale)* is a better bet, such as chops *(costolette)* with rosemary.

For **dessert**, fresh fruit might include strawberries *(fragole)*, a fruit salad *(macedonia di frutta)*, or fresh pears *(pere)* with creamy *gorgonzola* and *mascarpone* cheeses. In a truly *di lusso* (deluxe) establishment such as Capri's Hotel Quisisana, orange segments *(arance)* in orange liqueur may be prepared at your table with matchless Neapolitan flair: the waiter peels it in one unbroken spiral, then cuts out the segments, squeezes the juice from the membrane with a fork and arranges the segments like flower petals. If you want something a little more indulgent there's also a variety of more elaborate desserts such as *coviglie al caffè*, a rich, coffee-flavoured cream.

Naples' famous pastries are to be found in *pasticcerie* or bar/caffès, rather than on a restaurant's dessert menu. The mouth-watering selection of **cakes** include classic Campanian Easter cake *(pastiera)* made from fresh wheat grains, ricotta, and candied fruits; *sfogliatelle*, light, crisp pastries with various fillings, popular at breakfast time; and the incredibly sticky *struffoli*, like doughnuts drenched in honey.

Naples has long been famous for its delicious **ices** and **ice creams**, but it is more fun to sample these at a *gelateria*, where glorious pastries are also displayed. A *granita di caffè* or *limone* is a strongly flavoured ice shaved from frozen coffee or lemonade. Try the coffee *con panna* – with whipped cream.

Coffee

The beans for Italian coffee may come from the same sources as French, British, American or Turkish coffee, but what a difference! It's all in the roasting. Italian *espresso* is seemingly impossible to duplicate anywhere else, even with imported Italian *espresso* machines. With hot steam-foamed milk added to the cup and dusted with powdered chocolate, it's a *cappuccino*, brown and hooded like a Capuchin friar. With just a drop of hot milk it becomes a *caffè macchiata* (a 'stained' *espresso*).

WINES

The wines of Campania are rarely exported, though a recent surge in popularity may be changing that. Perhaps the best are the whites of Ischia, which are good

A chocolate-topped *cappuccino*

with seafood and *antipasti*, and Greco del Tufo, another dry white produced on the mainland, and the full-bodied Taurasi and Falerno reds. Capri produces small quantities of its own light, dry white wine, and even smaller amounts of red. Irpinia is an excellent local wine, available in red or white, and Ravello's red and rosé are renowned regionally. For every day, just say *rosso* to go with your pasta and you'll probably get a Gragnano. From the slopes of Vesuvius itself comes the mournfully named Lacryma Christi (Tears of Christ). The local house wine is usually a safe bet: see what the locals are ordering.

And at the end of the meal, have a digestif of icy cold limoncello, made from Amalfitana lemons and drunk straight from the freezer. *Buon appetito!*

To Help you Order…

I'd like a table. Vorrei un tavolo.
Do you have a set menu? Avete un menù a prezzo fisso?
I'd like… Vorrei…

beer	una birra	**pepper**	del pepe
bread	del pane	**potatoes**	delle patate
butter	del burro	**salad**	dell'insalata
coffee	un caffè	**salt**	del sale
cream	della panna	**soup**	una minestra
fork	una forchetta	**spoon**	un cucchiaio
glass	un bicchiere	**sugar**	dello zucchero
ice cream	un gelato	**tea**	un tè
knife	un coltello	**wine**	del vino

…and Read the Menu

acciughe	anchovies	**frutti di mare**	seafood
aglio	garlic	**funghi**	mushrooms
agnello	lamb	**gamberi**	prawns
albicocche	apricots	**limone**	lemon
arancia	orange	**melanzane**	aubergine
arrosto	roast	**maiale**	pork
braciola	chop	**peperoni**	peppers
calamari	squid	**pesca**	peach
calzone	folded pizza	**pesce**	fish
carciofi	artichokes	**pollo**	chicken
cipolle	onions	**polpi**	octopus
coniglio	rabbit	**pomodoro**	tomato
cozze	mussels	**salsa**	sauce
crostacei	shellfish	**sogliola**	sole
fagiolini	green beans	**spinaci**	spinach
fichi	figs	**tonno**	tuna
finocchio	fennel	**torta**	cake
formaggio	cheese	**uova**	eggs
frittata	omelette	**vongole**	clams

HANDY TRAVEL TIPS

An A–Z Summary of Practical Information

A

ACCOMMODATION (*Alloggio*; see also CAMPING; YOUTH HOSTELS)

The government-controlled star-rating system for accommodation descends from five to one. In Naples and the main resorts, amenities are spartan below three stars, but further afield more modest hotels and *pensioni* can be cosy bargains. Hotel recommendations are listed on *page 128*. For a good collection of online booking options, try <www.venere.com> or <www.bookings.com>. In season, don't rely on being able to get a room on arrival. You will, but not necessarily in the sort of hotel or at the sort of price you would like.

AIRPORT (*Aeroporto*)

Naples' airport is at Capodichino, located 5km (3 miles) from the city centre; tel: 081-7896259; fax 081-7896707; <www.gesac.it>. For flight information, tel: 081-7515471; lost baggage assistance, tel: 199 280 180. There is a major programme of redevelopment underway, due to be completed by the end of 2008.

There is limited duty-free shopping at the airport for travellers from outside the EU. International car-hire desks, regional and city tourist information offices and banking facilities are in the arrival area. Allow at least 20 minutes for the taxi ride from the airport to the centre of Naples (see BUDGETING FOR YOUR TRIP for fares). Bus line 3S and Alibus run regularly (every 20–30 mins) to Piazza Garibaldi and on to other city centre stops. Tickets can be purchased at the information desk in Arrivals or on the bus.

B

BICYCLE HIRE (*Noleggio di biciclette*)

Hiring a bicycle or scooter is possible in some resort towns and the islands. Some mechanics may rent you a scooter in Naples, but it is best to avoid this experience.

BUDGETING FOR YOUR TRIP

Here are some average prices in euros, based on high-season rates:

Airport transfer. Taxis from the airport into town charge double the fare on the meter, plus €0.30 per bag, plus €1 on Sundays and holidays. The average ride from the airport will cost around €30.

Camping. €3–8 per person per day.

Car hire. From €70 per day or €350 per week with unlimited mileage.

Entertainment. Cinema: €7. Concert: €10–40.

Guides (for 1–20 persons). Full day, €100; half day, €50.

Guided tours. Half-day trip to Pompeii, €45; full-day, Pompeii, Sorrento and Amalfi drive, €90, with lunch; boat to Blue Grotto, €15.

Meals and drinks. Continental breakfast, €4–15; lunch/dinner, €20–40; coffee €0.50 at the bar, €1.50 served at table; carafe of house wine from €3; beer €1.50; soft drink €1.50; aperitif €2–3.

Museums. €2–8. The Artecard offers free or discounted entry to museums in Naples or throughout the region, for 3, 7 or 365 days. Some include free transport. Prices range from €8–40. They are on sale at museums, tourist offices, newsagents, by calling 800-600 601 (tel: 06-399-67650 from abroad), or online at <www.campaniartecard.it>.

Transport. City bus and funicular, €1 per ride or €3 all-day ticket; metro, average ride €1; taxi, meter starts at €3, surcharges after 10pm and on Sundays and holidays; train to Pompeii, €3; boat to Capri or Ischia, €20 return; petrol, around €1.30 per litre. Unico 3T allows 72 hrs of travel on the rail system throughout Campania for €20 as well as city transport.

Youth Hostel. €15 person per night (without breakfast).

C

CAMPING *(Campeggio)*

There are campsites near Naples, by the Solfatara at Pozzuoli, all over the Phlegrean Fields and on the flanks of Vesuvius at Torre del Greco and Trecase, as well as near Sorrento, on Ischia and on the shore near

Paestum. Full details of sites are provided in the guide *Campeggi in Italia*, published annually by the Italian Touring Club (TCI). Federcampeggio's free list of sites, with location map, is available from tourist offices *(see page 126)* or from Federcampeggio (tel: 055-882391; <www.federcampeggio.it>). A list of campsites in Naples and surrounding areas can also be found at <www.camping.it/english/campania/napoli>. Most campsites are closed Nov–Apr. The Naples Complesso Turistico Averno site near the beach in Pozzuoli is open all year round (tel: 081-8042666). Campsites are jammed in summer, so it is a good idea to get the listings and phone ahead.

May we camp here?	**Possiamo campeggiare qui?**
Is there a campsite nearby?	**C'è un campeggio qui vicino?**

CAR HIRE (*Autonoleggio*; see also DRIVING)

Only a motoring masochist would choose to drive in Naples, where the public transport is excellent and the roads a nightmare, but driving in the countryside can be justified. All the major car-hire companies have agency windows in the arrival area of the airport and are listed in the yellow pages under *Autonoleggio*. Be sure to take a major credit card, since cash is often not accepted. Car hire is not cheap in Italy due to the high accident rate. Always check that the quoted rate includes Collision Damage Waiver, unlimited mileage and tax, as these can greatly increase the cost. Cheap deals may come with a huge excess. You must be over 21 to hire a car, and you will need to have held a full driving licence for at least 12 months.

I'd like to rent a car	**Vorrei noleggiare una macchina**
for tomorrow	**per domani**
for one day	**per un giorno**
for one week	**per una settimana**

CLIMATE

The weather in Naples and its nearby resorts is mild year-round. In July–August, the average high is 33°C (92°F), though heatwaves are not uncommon; the average minimum in January–February is 2°C (35°F). Spring comes early, with fruit trees blossoming in late March, and a golden autumn lingers into November. These are the best seasons to visit, mainly because they are less crowded. Mid-August, *ferragosto*, is when most Italian families take their holidays and the coastal areas are packed.

CLOTHING *(Abbigliamento)*

Italians are used to the informal dress of visitors. Few restaurants in Naples require a jacket and tie, though there are one or two elegant places where men might feel a bit out of place without them in the evening. As for the islands and coasts, pretty much anything goes, although shorts and barebacked dresses are frowned on in churches, and are not allowed in large cathedrals. Lightweight clothing is sufficient during most of the year, but from November to March the Bay of Naples can be damp and chilly between days of sunshine. Bring a raincoat and warm sweater in winter. A small foldup umbrella can come in handy at any season. You will need comfortable hiking shoes for climbing Vesuvius and exploring ruins. A hat is advisable as protection against the blazing summer sun.

COMPLAINTS *(Reclamo)*

In hotels, restaurants or shops complaints should be made to the manager. If you are still dissatisfied, threaten to make a formal declaration *(faccio la denuncia alla questura)* although carrying out this threat will be time consuming. To avoid problems, always establish prices in advance, especially when dealing with porters. For complaints about taxi fares, refer to the notice (in four languages) that is posted by law in each taxi, specifying extra charges (airport runs, Sunday or holiday rates, night surcharge) in excess of the meter rate.

CRIME AND SAFETY

Despite great improvement in the last 10 years and great strides made by the local government, Naples is still notorious for bag snatchers, break-ins and pickpockets. (Violent crime is common, too, but rarely affects tourists.) To prevent petty thieves from spoiling your holiday, carry no more cash than the minimum needed for transport, meals and tickets. Use credit cards for larger purchases. Carry your passport, credit cards, travellers' cheques, etc. in a pouch or zipped pocket inside your clothing. Don't carry a handbag or camera bag loosely slung over your street-side shoulder (thieves on motorbikes or in cars have been known to cut these off in Zorro-like drive-bys). Make photocopies of all documents and travellers' cheques to leave in your luggage in the eventuality of an actual theft and necessary replacement.

Never leave anything of value in your car when parked, not even in the boot; wherever possible, park in a garage or attended parking area. Never put items in the back window of a car, whether parked or in traffic. Leave valuables you don't need every day in the hotel safe; don't carry your hotel key with you outside the hotel. Don't wear conspicuous expensive jewellery; never let your bags out of sight in stations and public places. If you travel by train, keep the door and windows of sleeping-car compartments locked at night.

I want to report a theft.	**Voglio denunciare un furto.**
My wallet/handbag/	**Mi hanno rubato il portafoglio/**
passport/ticket	**la borsa/il passaporto/**
has been stolen.	**il biglietto.**

CUSTOMS AND ENTRY REQUIREMENTS

For a stay of up to three months, a valid passport is sufficient for citizens of Australia, Canada, New Zealand and USA. Visitors from EU countries need only an identity card to enter Italy. Tourists from South Africa must have a visa. Free exchange of non-duty-free goods for personal use is allowed between EU countries.

Currency restrictions. Tourists may bring an unlimited amount of Italian or foreign currency into the country. On departure, however, you must declare any currency beyond the equivalent of €10,000, so it's wise to declare sums exceeding this amount when you arrive.

Art. The Italian government is concerned about illegal traffic in art and archaeological relics; for such items you should obtain the proper documentation for export *(Nulla Oste)* from the dealer.

Pets. Dogs and cats must have a combined health and rabies inoculation certificate legalised by a vet. It must be dated between 11 months and 20 days before entry into Italy. An entry certificate will be valid for 30 days. Before taking your pet abroad, enquire about the quarantine regulations that may apply on your return home.

I've nothing to declare.	**Non ho niente da dichiarare.**
It's for my personal use.	**È per mio uso personale.**

D

DRIVING

Motorists planning to take their vehicle into Italy need a full driving licence with a translation (available from your automobile association), an International Motor Insurance Certificate and a Vehicle Registration Document. A green insurance card is not a legal requirement, but is strongly recommended. Full details are available from your automobile association or your insurance company.

The use of seat belts in front and back seats is obligatory; fines for non-compliance are stiff. A red warning triangle must be carried in case of breakdown. Motorcycle riders must wear crash helmets. The ACI (Automobile Club d'Italia; <www.aci.it>) gives some online information worth consulting before you set off.

Driving conditions. Drive on the right, and give way to traffic coming from the right. Speed limits: 50kph (30mph) in town, 90kph (55mph) on freeways *(superstrade)* and 130kph (80mph) on motorways *(autostrade)*. Few people stick to these however, and you will frequently find the locals doing a nerve-wracking 50kph (30mph) over the limit. Just try to stay out of their way. The *autostrade* are toll roads – take an entry ticket from a machine when you enter the motorway and pay at the other end for the distance travelled. On country roads you'll encounter bicycles, scooters, three-wheeled vehicles and horse-drawn carts. These slow-moving vehicles rarely have lights and are a danger after dark. The roads of the Sorrento peninsula are serpentine and filled with hire cars whose drivers are as unfamiliar with the road as you. Keep your eyes off the scenery and on the road. The Amalfi coast is so congested it becomes one-way in high summer and you have to drive right round the peninsula if you take a wrong turn.

Rules and regulations. Italian traffic police *(polizia stradale)* can impose on-the-spot fines for speeding and other traffic offences. All cities and many towns and villages have signs posted at the outskirts indicating the phone number of the local traffic police headquarters or *carabinieri* (see POLICE). Police have recently become stricter about speeding, an Italian national pastime, and are beginning to install hidden speed regulators with cameras.

Fuel. Petrol *(benzina)* is sold as Super and Unleaded *(senza piombo* or *SP)*. Diesel is called *gasolio*. It's illegal to carry spare fuel in your car. Petrol stations are generally open 7am–12.30pm and 3–7.30pm. Many have self-service (look for a '24' sign) via an automatic payment machine which accepts euro notes, and often credit/debit cards. Service stations on the *autostrada* are manned 24 hours a day.

Parking *(posteggio/parcheggio)*. In Naples, parking is so difficult and there are so few car parks that it is hardly worth looking for a place. Self-explanatory signs indicate tow-away zones *(zona di rimozione)* where parked cars will be whisked away in minutes. If this happens to you, find the nearest traffic policeman *(vigile urbano)*.

You can also call l'Ufficio Rimozione Auto (tel: 081-207191). At your request, white-capped parking attendants will take over your car and double or triple-park it in the bigger squares of the city, moving the cars like pieces of a puzzle when someone wants to get out.

Road signs. Most road signs in Italy are international. Here are some written signs you might also come across:

Curva pericolosa	Dangerous bend/curve
Deviazione	Detour
Divieto di sorpasso	No passing
Divieto di sosta	No stopping
Lavori in corso	Men working
Pericolo	Danger
Rallentare	Slow down
Senso vietato/unico	No entry/One-way street
Vietato l'ingresso	No entry
Zona pedonale	Pedestrian zone
ZTL	Limited traffic zone

Can I park here?	**Posso parcheggiare qui?**
Are we on the right road for...?	**Siamo sulla strada giusta per...?**
Please fill the tank with super/unleaded/diesel	**Per favore, faccia il pieno di super/senza piombo/gasolio**
I've had a breakdown.	**Ho avuto un guasto.**
There's been an accident.	**C'è stato un incidente.**

E

ELECTRICITY *(Elettricità)*

220v/50Hz AC is standard. The sockets are 2-round pin continental style but the pins are slimmer than some adapters on sale at airports; American 110v appliances also require a transformer.

| an adapter plug | **una presa complementare** |
| a voltage transformer | **un trasformatore** |

EMBASSIES AND CONSULATES *(Ambasciate; Consolati)*

Australia: Via Antonio Bosio 5, Rome, tel: 06-852721, fax: 06-852 72300, toll-free (for serious emergencies only): 800 877 790, <www. italy.embassy.gov.au>.

Canada: Via Carducci 29, Naples, tel: 081-401338, fax: 081-410 4210, email: <cancons.nap@tiscalinet.it>, <www.canada.it>.

New Zealand: Via Zara 28, Rome, tel: 06-441 7171, fax: 06-440 2984, email: <nzemb.rom@flashnet.it>, <www.nzembassy.com>.

Republic of Ireland: Piazza Campitelli 3, Rome, tel: 06-697 9121.

South Africa: Via Stendhal 23, Naples, tel: 081-552 5835, fax: 081-551 4036, email: <consular@sudafrica.it>, <www.sudafrica.it>.

UK: Via dei Mille 40, Naples, tel: 081-4238911, fax: 081-422434, email: <info.naples@fco.gov.uk>, <www.britain.it>.

US: Piazza della Republica, Naples, tel: 081-5838111, fax: 081-7611869, <www.usembassy.it>.

EMERGENCIES *(Emergenza)*

The numbers to dial in emergencies are:

Carabinieri	112	General emergency	113
Fire	115	Ambulance	118

If you don't speak Italian, find a local resident to help you, or talk to an English-speaking operator by dialling **170**.

Can you please place an	**Per favore, può fare una**
emergency call...	**telefonata d'emergenza...**
to the police?	**alla polizia?**
to the fire brigade?	**ai vigili del fuoco?**
to the hospital?	**all'ospedale?**

G

GAY AND LESBIAN TRAVELLERS

Naples is as gay-friendly as any of Italy's large cities – which is to say relatively. The coastline resort areas have long attracted gay northern-Italian holidaymakers from the fashion and art worlds, particularly Positano and Capri. Arcigay, the national gay rights organisation is a great source for finding bars, beaches and other localities that are particularly gay-friendly. Contact Arcigay Napoli, Via San Geronimo alle Monache 19, tel: 081-552 8815, <www.arcigay napoli.org>; open Mon–Fri 4.30pm–8pm and Sat 10.30am–1.30pm. Also try <www.gay.it> for updated information. The magazine *Spartacus International Gay Guide* is available at the newsstands.

GETTING THERE

By air. Capodichino Airport is served by direct flights from many European cities, including London Stansted, Gatwick and Manchester, through British Airways <www.ba.com>, bmi <www.fly bmi.com>, easyJet <www.easyjet.com> and Thomsonfly <www.thomsonfly.com>. In summer, charter flights add to the schedule. From the US, there are direct flights from New York with Eurofly <www.eurofly.it>, or you can fly via Rome or Milan.

By rail. Naples is on the fast European sleeper and express train lines, with through trains to major Italian cities, European capitals and almost hourly connections with Rome.

By car. Rome is 220km (137 miles) away by *autostrada* (motorway).

By coach. In addition to the very comprehensive, inexpensive, but rather slow intercity bus services linking Naples to the rest of Italy, express coaches from Rome serve Naples and, in the summer, Sorrento and Positano as well. Consult the CIT, Piazza Municipio 72, Naples; tel: 081-5525426; fax: 081-5521378; email <citnapoli@cititalia.net>. Coach tours to the region are operated by tour operators in most European countries. National Express Eurolines runs coaches from London Victoria to Naples (tel: 08705 808080 in the UK; to book in Italy, tel: 055-357110; <www.eurolines.com>).

By sea. If your destination is an island or seaside resort, speedy hydrofoil services and fast passenger ferries leave Naples regularly from the Molo Beverello docks in the Castel Nuovo district and Mergellina harbour near the train station of the same name. The trip to Capri, Ischia or Sorrento takes 30–60 mins. Larger car ferries also leave for Sicily's Aeolian Islands and Palermo, Sardinia and Tunisia. They are run by a profusion of different companies, so you it is best to ask a local travel agent or at the Molo Beverello ticket office.

GUIDES AND TOURS

Guided tours of Naples and the surrounding area can be arranged through Giro Città', tel: 081-2470006. Guides who offer services at tourist sites, such as Pompeii or the National Archaeological Museum, should be asked to show their credentials. Every Saturday and Sunday the official Naples tourist organisation conducts three tours of a different church or site. For information, Contact LAES, tel: 081-400256, <www.lanapolisotteranea.it>. City Sightseeing Napoli (tel: 081-551 7279, <www.napoli.city-sightseeing.it>) operates a hop-on, hop-off bus with commentary in eight languages; tickets last 24hrs.

H

HEALTH AND MEDICAL CARE

EU residents should obtain the European Health Insurance Card, available in the UK from post offices or online <www.ehic.org.uk>, which entitles them to emergency medical treatment. To cover all eventualities, medical insurance is recommended. Non-EU visitors must pay for medical care and medicine, and should have medical insurance.

Public hospitals in Naples tend to be overcrowded, and you may prefer private care. Ask your consulate or hotel to recommend an English- speaking doctor or dentist, or a clinic.

Chemists *(farmacie)* follow shop hours and close for lunch, but they take turns as the *farmacia di turno*, open night and day. The addresses of pharmacies on duty appear on every chemist's door and in local papers. In Italy, pharmacists can often provide medication which at home would normally require a prescription. So, in anything but an emergency, try visiting the chemist before rushing to hospital.

Where's the nearest (all-night) pharmacy?	**Dov'è la farmacia (di turno) più vicina?**
I need a doctor/dentist.	**Ho bisogno di un medico/dentista.**
a stomach ache	**un mal di stomaco**
a fever	**la febbre**

HOLIDAYS

Banks, government offices, most shops and some museums and galleries are closed on the following days. When one falls on a Thursday or a Tuesday, Italians may make a *ponte* (bridge) to the weekend, meaning that Friday or Monday is taken off as well.

I January	*Capodanno*	New Year's Day
6 January	*Epifania*	Epiphany
25 April	*Festa della Liberazione*	Liberation Day
I May	*Festa del Lavoro*	Labour Day
14 May	*San Costanzo*	St Constance (Capri)
13 June	*San Antonio*	St Anthony (Anacapri)
15 August	*Ferragosto*	Assumption Day
19 September	*San Gennaro*	Patron Saint of Naples
I November	*Ognissanti*	All Saint's Day
8 December	*L'Immacolata Concezione*	Immaculate Conception
25 December	*Natale*	Christmas Day
26 December	*Santo Stefano*	St Stephen's Day
Movable dates	*Pasqua*	Easter Sunday
	Lunedì di Pasqua	Easter Monday

L

LANGUAGE

Your effort to speak a few words of Italian will win smiles and cooperation. Also, many Italians are studying English and are keen to try it out on visitors. The Neopolitan dialect is impenetrable, even to northern Italians. Bear in mind the following tips on Italian pronunciation:

c   is pronounced like *ch* in 'charge' when followed by an *e* or an *i*, as in *cello* = 'chello' and *arriverderci* = 'ariverder-chee'

ch sounds like *k*

g   followed by an *e* or an *i* has a *j* sound, as in 'jet'

gh sounds like *g* in 'go'

gl followed by *i* sounds like *lli* in 'million'

gn is pronounced like *ny* in 'canyon', eg *gnocchi* = 'nyaw-kee'

sc before *e* and *i* is pronounced *sh* as in 'ship'

The Berlitz Italian Phrase Book and Dictionary covers all the situations you are likely to encounter in Italy; it includes a pronunciation guide, basic grammar and 3,500-word dictionary.

Do you speak English?	**Parla inglese?**
I don't speak Italian.	**Non parlo italiano.**

LAUNDRY AND DRY-CLEANING *(Lavanderia; Tintoria)*

Most hotels will do laundry the same day and dry-cleaning overnight, although this is more expensive than using a launderette or drycleaner. Naples has two self-service launderettes: Corso Novara (near Stazione Centrale) and My Beautiful Launderette (Via Monte Santo).

When will it be ready?	**Quando sarà pronto?**
I must have this for tomorrow morning.	**Mi serve perdomani mattina.**

M

MAPS

There are so many tiny alleys in Naples, they can't all fit on a map, or at least on the ones you can get free from the Information Office on Piazza del Gesú. Many maps of the area can be found at newsstands and bookshops, including the excellent Touring Club of Italy maps.

> I'd like a street map of…   **Vorrei una piantina di…**

MEDIA

Newspapers and Magazines (*giornali, riviste*). In Naples, the kiosks run out of foreign publications early. If you are staying here for some time and want your favourite paper regularly, order it or ask your hotel to do so. In Capri the kiosk in the central Piazzetta has a good selection, and the same is true in other resort towns. The free monthly *Qui Napoli*, a compilation of all visitor-necessary information, is distributed in most hotels and through the different visitor centres.

Radio and TV (*radio, televisione*). The Italian state TV network, RAI, has three TV channels, which compete with six independent channels. All programmes are in Italian, including British and American programmes and feature films, which are dubbed. CNN (in English) is transmitted on TMC in the morning 4.20–6am and from 3.15am on Sundays. Most hotels and hired properties have cable connections which show CNN Europe and CNBC all day. The airwaves are crammed with radio stations, most broadcasting popular music. The nearby NATO base broadcasts English programmes all day on 106 and 107FM.

MONEY (*Denaro*)

Currency. Italy's currency is the euro. Notes are denominated in 5, 10, 20, 50, 100 and 500 euros; coins in 1 and 2 euros and 1, 2, 5, 10, 20 and 50 cents.

Banks and currency exchange *(banca; ufficio di cambio)*. Banks give the best exchange rates, and the transaction is usually rapid and courteous. Don't forget to take along your passport when changing travellers' cheques. Exchange offices are an alternative virtually as good as banks and with longer hours.

ATMs. Drawing money from ATMs (cash dispensers) on your credit or debit card usually offers the best exchange rate.

Credit cards are widely accepted in the Naples area. The cards accepted are usually indicated on the door. Don't expect cards to be accepted by market traders, small village shops and some trattorias.

Travellers' cheques can be used for purchases, but they are becoming less common, and you will get much better value if you exchange your cheques for euros at a bank or *cambio*.

I want to change some pounds/dollars/ travellers' cheques.	**Desidero cambiare delle sterline/dei dollari/ travellers' cheque.**
Can I pay with this credit card?	**Posso pagare con la carta di credito?**
Where is the bank?	**Dov'è la banca?**
Where is an ATM?	**Dov'è il bancomat?**

OPENING HOURS *(Orari di apertura)*

Banks are generally open Mon–Fri 8.30am–1.30pm, reopening later for an hour, 3–4pm. The currency exchange office at Stazione Centrale is open daily 8am–8pm.

Shops are usually open from 8.30 or 9am to 12.30 or 1pm, then from 3.30 or 4 to 7.30pm or later. Many shops are closed on Mondays, especially in winter, and sometimes Saturday afternoons in summer. In resorts, hours will be stretched to fit high season demand.

Churches close for most of the afternoon, reopening around 5pm, but the biggest churches may remain open all day. Museum hours are generally 9am–1pm with late afternoon opening from around 3–6pm, six days a week; closed Mondays. However, there are so many variations between seasons, among museums, and even within galleries of a museum that you should check with the tourist information office before planning your day.

P

POLICE

In town, the *vigili urbani*, in blue or summer white uniforms with white hats, handle traffic and routine tasks. The *carabinieri*, dressed in brown or black uniforms, maintain law and order throughout the country. Their headquarters, the Questura, deals with visas and other complaints, and is a good point of reference if you need help from the authorities. The motorways are patrolled by the *polizia stradale*. Another corps of national police and customs guards are on duty at frontier posts, airports and railway stations.

In an emergency, dial **112** or **113** for police assistance.

Where's the nearest police station?	**Dov'è il commissariato di polizia più vicino?**

POST OFFICES (Posta)

Look for the yellow sign with *PT* in black. Normal post office hours are 8.30am–2pm, Mon–Fri, closing at noon on Saturday and the last day of the month. The Naples main post office on Via Armando Diaz is open 8am–6pm Mon–Fri and 8am–1pm Sat. Post boxes on the streets are painted red; the slot marked 'Per la Città' is for local mail, while the other labeled 'Altre Destinazioni' is for all other destinations. Stamps *(francobolli)* can also be bought at tobacconists and at some hotels. Ask for *Posta Prioritaria*, an express service which costs a little more but gets to its destination much faster.

Where's the nearest post office?	**Dov'è l' ufficio postale più vicino?**
A stamp for this letter/ postcard, please.	**Un francobollo per questa lettera/cartolina, per favore.**
airmail	**via aerea**
registered	**raccomandata**

PUBLIC TRANSPORT

Naples has an excellent integrated transport network of metros (subways/undergrounds), bus lines, trams, funiculars and suburban railways, as well as ferries and numerous taxis, that will get you close to wherever you want to go in the city and surrounding points of interest. Get a good map and bus timetables from a local tourist information office. Be aware of the infamous Italian *sciopero* or transport strikes that can last from a few hours to a few days. Try to check with your hotel before going out for the day as they are always announced and publicised in the paper and on the news. Always remember to punch the time on all tickets, otherwise you will risk a stiff fine.

Bus. 90-minute or all-day tickets valid for unlimited bus, metro and funicular travel are available in Naples (see BUDGETING FOR YOUR TRIP for costs). Capri's bus terminal for Anacapri and the two harbours is on Via Roma, just beyond the main square. In Ischia town the round-the-island buses leave from a parking area to the right of the harbour. Tickets may be purchased from ticket offices in the terminals.

Metro. Naples' subway system runs on the same underground tracks as the railway. It links up with the Circumflegrea and Cumana lines for Pozzuoli and the Phlegrean Fields sites at the Montesanto Station. There it also connects with a funicular to the Vomero district. A metro line also connects Vomero to the city centre and other lines are under construction. The same tickets used for buses are valid on these lines. Tickets for the Circumvesuviana line trains to Ercolano (Herculaneum), Pompeii and Sorrento picked up at the Piazza Garibaldi's Central Station, are charged separately according to the distance travelled.

Taxis *(tassi or taxi)*. In Naples taxis can be found at a taxi rank, hailed or ordered by telephone. The numbers for all the Naples ranks are in the *Qui Napoli* bulletin and can be called by your hotel or from a restaurant. A flag marked *libero* and a roof light at night indicate free taxis. For long trips out of town, taxis are entitled to charge a double fare for returning empty. Negotiate and confirm before undertaking such a trip, or have your hotel concierge do so. It is normal practice to round up the fare.

Trains *(treni)*. Children under the age of 4 travel free (unless individual accommodation is required); children aged 4 to 12 pay half fare. Apart from providing one of Europe's lowest regular fares, the Italian State Railways offer several reduced rates. Tickets can be purchased and reservations made at travel agencies and railway stations. For train information dial 89 20 21 (a local call throughout Italy; English-speaking operators) or visit <www.trenitalia.com>.

Italian trains are classified according to speed. Best and fastest are the Eurostar (first and second class; require seat reservations) which have their own ticketing windows at all stations. They are further classified as Intercity (IC; first and second class; often require seat reservations to be made one day before) and the Espresso (E; first and second class; often require seat reservations). The Diretto (D) makes a number of local stops, and there are the two local trains InterRegionale (IR; first and second class) and Regionale (REG; second class only); both tend to be very slow.

In Naples, trains to international and national destinations (other than the Cumana and Circumflegrea suburban lines) leave from the Stazione Centrale in the Piazza Garibaldi and Mergellina station.

Ferries *(traghetti)*. Ferries and hydrofoils *(aliscafi)* to the islands, Sorrento, Amalfi coastal towns and Salerno, leave frequently from the Molo Beverello pier at the foot of the Piazza -Municipio and from the Mergellina dock, starting at around 6am until around 9pm. Hydrofoils and ferries are operated by several companies. The information number for the Caremar line is 081-5513882. There are overnight ferries to Sicily's Aeolian Islands, Palermo, Sardinia and Tunisia.

When's the next bus/ train/boat for…?	**A che ora parte il prossimo autobus/treno/traghetto per…?**
What's the fare to…?	**Quanto costa il biglietto per…?**
I want a ticket to…	**Vorrei un biglietto per…**
single (one-way)	**andata**
return (round-trip)	**andata e ritorno**
first/second class	**prima/seconda classe**
I'd like to make seat reservations.	**Vorrei prenotare un posto.**
Will you tell me when to get off?	**Può dirmi quando devo scendere?**

R

RELIGION *(Religione)*

Needless to say, there is no shortage of Roman Catholic services daily in every Naples neighbourhood and in the resort communities. In Naples, the Anglican Church at Via San Pasquale 18 in Chiaia has Sunday services at 8am and 10am; tel: 081-411842. The Synagogue in Via Santa Maria a Cappella Vecchia off the Piazza dei Martiri holds services on Fridays at sunset and at 8.30am on Saturdays; tel: 081-764 3480. For Protestant services in Italian, see the monthly *Qui Napoli* bulletin available in the Piazza del Gesù Information Office.

Is there a … near here?	C'è una … qui vicino?
Catholic/Protestant church/	chiesa cattolica/protestante/
mosque/synagogue	moschea/sinagoga
What time is the service?	A che ora è la funzione?

T

TELEPHONE *(Telefono)*

Most Italians now have mobile phones glued to their ears (European standard GSM, so Americans will need a tri- or quad-band phone) so public telephones *(cabina telefonica)* are fairly scarce. However, you can also phone from bars and cafés with an orange telephone sign outside. Overseas and other calls requiring assistance can be made from any Telecom Italia office called Punto Telecom. In Naples, long-distance calls can be made from the main post office and on Capri there is a long-distance telephone office (open 8–11.30am and 3–11pm) adjoining the clock tower in the Piazzetta.

Most public telephones now accept only phonecards *(scheda telefonica)*, available in different denominations from tobacconists and Telecom Italia offices. There are also pre-paid international phone cards, with toll-free numbers for different countries. To make an international call, dial 00, followed by the country code.

If you want to make a reverse-charge (collect) call, you must often insert a coin or a card to access a line (even for toll-free calls). Hotels often charge exorbitantly and add 'service charges' for toll-free calls.

These English-speaking services operate 24 hours a day:

International operator: **170**

International directory enquiries: **176**

| Give me coins/ | **Per favore, mi dia monette/** |
| a telephone card, please. | **una scheda telefonica.** |

TICKETS

Advance tickets for any performances and events can often be arranged through the concierge of the better hotels or can be bought at the following agencies:

Box Office: Galleria Umberto I, Naples; tel: 081-551 9188; fax: 081-551 0297. Tickets for the opera at Teatro San Carlo opposite.

Concerteria: Via M. Schipa 23, Naples; tel: 081-761 1221; fax: 081-761 2231.

TIME ZONE *(Fuso orario)*

Italy follows Central European Time (GMT+1) and from late March to the last weekend in October, clocks are put ahead one hour.

New York	London	**Naples**	Jo'burg	Sydney	Auckland
6am	11am	**noon**	noon	8pm	10pm

What time is it?	**Che ora è?**

TIPPING *(Mancia)*

A service charge of approximately 15 percent is added to restaurant bills. If prices are quoted as all-inclusive *(tutto compreso or servizio incluso)* the service charge is included, but not necessarily the IVA (20 percent VAT/sales tax); ask if you're not sure. In addition to a restaurant's service charge, it is customary to give the waiter something extra, preferably in cash. Porters, doormen, bartenders and service-station attendants all expect a tip. Rounding up your taxi fare to the next euro will satisfy your driver.

Thank you, this is for you.	**Grazie, questo è per Lei.**
Keep the change.	**Tenga il resto.**

TOILETS

Toilets may be labelled with a symbol of a man or a woman or the initials WC. Sometimes the wording will be in Italian, but beware, as you might be misled: *Uomini* is for men, *Donne* is for women. But also, *Signori* (with a final *i*) is for men, *Signore* (with an *e*) is for women. Only rarely will you still find the squatting type of hole in the floor; head for the lobby of a large hotel if you want to avoid this. Always have a packet of tissues in your pocket, just in case the toilet you come upon is not properly stocked.

Where are the toilets?	**Dove sono i gabinetti?**

TOURIST INFORMATION

The standard symbol for information offices is an italic lower-case '*i*.' All resort towns have one in a central location. In **Naples**, there is a well-equipped office in the Piazza del Plebiscito, opposite the Palazzo Reale (tel: 081-252 5711). Others are at the Piazza del Gesù, Mergellina dock, the Castel dell'Ovo and in the centre of the Piazza Garibaldi in front of the Central Station. The office serving the province of Campania is located at Piazza dei Martiri 58. In the Capodichino Airport arrival hall both the city and provincial organisations have stands that provide brochures and maps, as does an information office on the upper concourse of the Central Railway Station. In **Capri** the tiny tourist office is in the belltower at the corner of the town square. On **Ischia** it is to the right of the dock. In **Positano** it is behind the beachfront cafés at Via del Saracino 4. In **Sorrento**, it is beside the ferry port. Everywhere, just ask for the Ufficio di Turismo.

The Italian State Tourist Offices (ENIT; <www.enit.it>) are found in Italy and abroad. They publish detailed brochures with relatively up-to-date information on accommodation, transport and other general tips and addresses for the whole country.

Australia and New Zealand: Level 26, 44 Market Street, Sydney, NSW 2000, tel: (02) 9262 1666, fax: (02) 9262 1677, email: <eni tour@ihug.com.au>.
Canada: 175 Bloor Street East, Suite 907, South Tower, Toronto, Ontario M4W 3R8, tel: (416) 925 4882, fax: (416) 925 4799.
UK: 1 Princes Street, London W1B 2AY, tel: (020) 7408 1254, fax: (020) 7399 3567, email: <italy@italiantouristboard.co.uk>; <www.italiantouristboard.co.uk>.
US: 630 Fifth Avenue, Suite 1565, New York, NY 10111, tel: (212) 245 5618, fax: (212) 586 9249, email: <enitny@italiantourism.com>, <www.italiantourism.com>.

WEIGHTS AND MEASURES

Like most of Europe, Italy uses the metric system:

1 metre	=	approx 39 ins
1 kilometre	=	1,093 yards or approx 0.6 mile
16km	=	approx 10 miles
1 kilogram	=	approx 2.2 lb
1 litre	=	1.75 pints
40 litres	=	approx 9 gallons (10 US gallons)

YOUTH HOSTELS *(Ostello della gioventù)*

There is one youth hostel in Naples: Ostella Mergellina Napoli, Salita della Grotta 23; tel: 081-7612346; fax: 081-7612391. It is available for members of the International Youth Hostels Federation. Book well in advance. Information is available from the Associazione Italiana Alberghi per la Gioventù (AIG), the Italian Youth Hostels Association, at Via Cavour 44, 00184 Rome; tel: (06) 487 1152; fax: (06) 488 0492; <www.ostellionline.org>.

Recommended Hotels

Italian hotels are classified by the government from five stars down to one star according to the facilities they offer, though the star rating does not give a guide to the character or location of the hotel. Prices nearly always include breakfast, but check when you book. As a basic guide we have used the symbols below to indicate prices per night for a double room with bath or shower, including service charge and taxes, during the high season. Prices may be considerably lower in the off-season (generally November to mid-March), although most resort hotels close then. Keep in mind that rooms with sea views generally cost more. In the coastal resorts, it is not unusual to find that half-board is compulsory in high season. All of the hotels listed accept major credit cards except where noted.

€€€€	250 euros and above
€€€	180–250 euros
€€	125–180 euros
€	below 125 euros

NAPLES

Holiday Inn €€ *Centro Direzionale Isola E6, 80143, tel: 081-225 0111, <www.ihg.com>.* Perhaps not the most exciting hotel in town and out near the business district, but convenient for the airport, great value for money, comfortable and friendly, with free shuttle services to the city centre, station and airport. 330 rooms.

Majestic €€ *Largo Vasto a Chiaia 68, 80121, tel: 081-416500, fax: 081-410145, <www.majestic.it>.* This grand old-world style hotel was built in 1960. Its 1999 renovation has refreshed it, explaining its popularity with business folk. Many appreciate its well-frequented restaurant 'La Giara', modern rooms, and the hotel's proximity to both the historical and commercial centre. 116 rooms.

Parker's €€€€ *Corso Vittorio Emanuele 135, 80121, tel: 081-7612474, fax: 081-663527, <www.grandhotelparkers.it>.* Founded more than 130 years ago, this grand hotel is away from the waterfront in fashionable Chiaia. The rooftop George's Restaurant and Bar offers candlelit dining at night, heart-stopping views of Vesuvius and Capri by day. 81 rooms and suites.

Piazza Bellini €€ *Via S Maria di Costantinopoli 101, 80134, tel/fax: 081-451732, <www.hotelpiazzabellini.com>.* A small boutique hotel growing up fast, this charming establishment in one of Naples' trendiest piazzas, on the edge of the old city, only opened recently and is expanding rapidly. Rooms are spacious, understated and slightly funky. Staff are delightful. 50 rooms.

Santa Lucia €€€ *Via Partenope 46, 80121, tel: 081-764 0666, fax: 081-764 8580, <www.santalucia.it>.* The picturesque port is the timeless view enjoyed by many of the rooms in one of Naples' loveliest hotels. Directly across from the Castel dell'Ovo. 100 rooms.

Soggiorno Sansevero € *Piazza San Domenico Maggiore 9, 80138, tel: 081-790 1000, <www.albergosansevero.it>* Basking in the heart of atmospheric Spaccanapoli, this small family-run hotel is simple but clean and charming. There are three other properties in the group if you can't get in here. 11 rooms.

Vesuvio €€€€ *Via Partenope 45, 80121, tel: 081-764044, fax: 081-764044, <www.vesuvio.it>.* A glorious grande-dame of a hotel, the Vesuvio stares serenely out across Santa Lucia and the bay. Caruso, the wonderful roof-garden restaurant, is named after the Neapolitan tenor, who was a frequent guest. There is also a sumptuous spa. 179 rooms.

CAPRI

Palace €€€€ *Via Capodimonte 2b, Anacapri 80071, tel: 081-837 3800, fax: 081-837 3191, <www.capripalace.com>.* Anacapri's seclusion, top-rate beauty and health centre, and award-winning cuisine are the magnets at the island's most luxurious hotel. The large pool and luxuriant gardens are highlights; the views, on a clear day, stretch to Mt Vesuvius. 115 rooms. Open April to October.

Quisisana €€€€ *Via Camerelle 2, Capri Town 80073, tel: 081-837 0788, fax: 081-837 6080, <www.quisi.it>.* An oasis in the centre of town, for decades the island's most fabled hotel. Luxurious rooms with sea views, manicured gardens, indoor and outdoor pools, gym, spa and tennis. Outdoor dining; the trendy front-porch bar is a must-do for a drink. 150 rooms.

Regina Cristina €€€ *Via Serena 20, Capri Town 80073, tel: 081-837 0744, fax: 081-837 0550, <www.reginacristina.com>.* Pricey, but with the island's slim pickings, it's open all year. Every room is bright and airy with its own balcony, some overlooking the hotel's lovely garden or pool. 55 rooms.

Villa Krupp € *Via Matteotti 12, Capri Town 80073, tel: 081-837 0362, fax: 081-837 6489.* Overlooking the Gardens of Augustus, this was once home to Russian revolutionary Maxim Gorky (and his guest Lenin). Some rooms have views of wooded hills and glimpses of the cobalt-blue sea. Staying here involves walking and climbing steep stairs. 12 rooms. Open end of March to October.

Villa Sarah €€ *Via Tiberio 3/a, Capri Town 80073, tel: 081-837 7817, fax: 081-837 7215, <www.villasarah.it>.* Centrally located yet removed from the hubbub, this is a quiet, clean family-run hotel with contemporary rooms and a beautiful shady garden. A few rooms on upper floors face the sea. 20 rooms. Open from Easter to September.

ISCHIA

Grand Hotel Excelsior Terme €€ *Via Emanuele Gianturco 19, Ischia Porto 80077, tel: 081-991522, fax: 081-984100, email: <excelsior@leohotels.it>, <www.excelsiorischia.it>.* Once the 19th-century home of an English nobleman, a palatial hotel in peaceful woods near its own private beach. Public areas and spacious rooms are in elegant period style. Heated pool, spa, garden and terraced restaurant. 78 rooms. Open late April to October.

Il Monastero € *Castello Aragonese 3, Ischia Ponte 80070, tel: 081-992435, fax: 081-991849, email: <ilmonastero@castelloaragonese.it>,*

<www.albergoilmonastero.it>. Old monastery within the Castello Aragonese converted into a good-value *pensione*. Rooms are simple but attractive, some of them opening on to the terrace, with stunning sea views. Good restaurant. 22 rooms. Open April to October.

Punta Molino Terme €€€ *Lungomare C. Colombo 23, Ischia Porto 80070, tel: 081-991544, fax: 081-991562, <www.puntamolino.it>*. A modern resort compound in a vast pine park that contains three pools, a private beach with water sports, a beauty and spa centre, and respected restaurants. Amid the formal elegance are many island crafts by top local artisans. 90 rooms. Open April to October.

Hotel Terme San Michele € *Via Sant'Angelo 60, Sant'Angelo 80070, tel: 081-999276, fax: 081-999149, <www.hoteltermesan michele.it>*. A shady oasis surrounds this modern waterside hotel with a large pool, pretty gardens, shady terraces, a full-scale beauty centre for thermal water and mud treatments. Tasteful guest rooms, many with balconies and sea views. Half board in the busy restaurant is compulsory. 40 rooms. Open April to October.

SORRENTO

Crowne Plaza Stabiae €€ *SS 145 Sorrentina, km11, Castellammare di Stabia, 80053, tel: 081-394 6700, <www.sorrentocoast hotel.com>*. An old cement works imaginatively converted into a stylish resort hotel with a fine pool and spa near Vico Equense on the Sorrento coast. Getting here is a little problematic, but the food alone is worth it – some of the best in the bay area. 152 rooms.

Grand Hotel Excelsior Vittoria €€€€ *Piazza Tasso 34, 80067, tel: 081-807 1044, fax: 081-877 1206, <www.exvitt.it>*. An elegant cliff-top belle époque dream, awash with *trompe l'oeil*, potted plants, and gorgeous views over Vesuvius and the bay. This lovely small hotel was once home to the great Caruso (with his suite available for special bookings). Secluded but in the very heart of town, with a semi-tropical garden, large swimming pool, and a lift to take bathers down to the sea. Formal indoor and terraced alfresco restaurant with views, holistic spa. 106 rooms.

Imperial Tramontano €€€ *Via Vittorio Veneto 1, 80067, tel: 081-878 2588, fax: 081-807 2344, <www.hoteltramontano.it>*. Parts of this villa-like hotel date from the 15th century. Perched on a cliff and surrounded by subtropical gardens, it has a freshwater swimming pool, spacious ceramic-tiled rooms, some with superb views of the Bay of Naples. Private beach and a restaurant run by master-chef, Don Alfonso. 116 rooms. Open March to December.

La Badia € *Via Nastro Verde 8, Sorrento 80067, tel: 081-878 1154, fax: 081-807 4159, <www.hotellabadia.it>*. A delightful little restored abbey surrounded by citrus groves, on the clifftops above Sorrento town. Pool, restaurant and fabulous views. It's a steep walk but there are regular buses. 40 rooms.

La Tonnarella €€ *Via del Capo 31, 80067, tel: 081-878 1153, fax: 081-878 2169, <www.latonnarella.it>*. This clifftop villa is a good value choice, and one of only a few on the coast open all year. A quiet hideaway, a 10-minute walk into town. Excellent restaurant; a few rooms with pine-shaded terracotta balconies and panoramic views of the bay; small private pebble beach with bar reached by lift. 22 rooms.

POSITANO

Casa Albertina €€€ *Via della Tavolozza 3, 84017, tel: 089-875143, fax: 089-811540, <www.casalbertina.it>*. This pretty family-owned guesthouse is not for the weak of knee: there are 300 steps down to the beach, but it has exceptional views. Some rooms with balconies and Jacuzzis. Compulsory half-board in high season. 20 rooms.

Covo dei Saraceni €€€€ *Via Regina Giovanna 5, 84017, tel: 089-875400, fax: 089-875878, <www.covodeisaraceni.it>*. If you were any closer to the sea you'd be in it. Rather luxe, this long-time favourite has cool, crisp and stylish rooms with seaview balconies; many have Jacuzzis. A delightful rooftop pool and bar and a fine terrace restaurant. 61 rooms. Open mid-March to 7 January.

Miramare €€€ *Via Trara Genoino 27, 84017, tel: 089-875002, fax: 089-875219, <www.miramarepositano.it>*. It's a short climb from the beach to this small, charming cliffside hotel, converted from two old private houses and furnished with personal touches. Delightful rooms have balconies with sea views, and the public rooms are beautifully furnished with a mix of antiques. 15 rooms. Open April to October.

Palazzo Murat €€€€ *Via dei Mulini 23, 84017, tel: 089-875177, fax: 089-811419, <www.palazzomurat.it>*. Elegant and romantic town-centre hotel in a 19th-century palazzo furnished with antiques. The slightly cheaper Mediterranean-style wing is surrounded by a quiet subtropical courtyard. Good restaurant (dinner only). 32 rooms. Open mid-March until early January.

Poseidon €€€ *Via Pasitea 148, 84017, tel: 089-811111, fax: 089-875833, <www.hotelposeidonpositano.it>*. The Aonzo family proudly runs this hillside hotel, one of Positano's nicest and most popular, with pool, beauty centre, gym and good restaurant. Removed from the day-tripping buzz yet accessible to everything. All rooms have terraces and lovely views. 52 rooms. Open early April to 6 January.

San Pietro €€€€ *Via Laurito 82, 84017, tel: 089-875455, fax: 089-811449, <www.ilsanpietro.it>*. An A-listers' hideaway with a dozen levels of vine-covered balconies chiselled into the cliff above a private helipad, this stunning, secluded family-owned hotel offers a mix of refined elegance and airy, contemporary decor. Stylish restaurant, spa, small, rocky private beach. 60 rooms. Open April to October.

La Sirenuse €€€€ *Via C. Colombo 30, 84017, tel: 089-875066, fax: 089-811798, <www.sirenuse.it>*. In an aristocratic 18th-century building in town above the beach, this is one of the country's most special hotels. Museum-quality family heirlooms throughout, wonderful open views of the sea and town, new stylish health centre, outdoor pool, refined restaurant. 60 rooms.

RAVELLO

Palazzo Sasso €€€€ *Via San Giovanni del Toro 28, 84010, tel: 089-818181, fax: 089-858900, <www.palazzosasso.com>*. This 12th-century aristocratic home has a gorgeous cliff-top setting. One of the most fashionable and chic hotels around. Rooms are expensive, but they all have breathtaking sea views and are worth the premium. The food at the two-Michelin-star Rossellini restaurant is magnificent. 43 rooms. Open March to October.

Villa Cimbrone €€€ *Via Santa Chiara 26, 84010, tel: 089-857459, fax: 089-857777, <www.villacimbrone.it>*. The suite Greta Garbo stayed in is part of this magical old palazzo. Vaulted, frescoed rooms filled with an eclectic mix of antiques belonging to the former British owner's family. The enchanting gardens suspended above the sea are for hotel guests alone once the grounds close at dusk. Located at the end of a 15-minute trek along a charming footpath; porters will help guests with luggage. 13 rooms. Open April to October.

AMALFI

La Bussola €€ *Lungomare dei Cavalieri 18, 84011, tel: 089-871533, fax: 089-871369, <www.labussolahotel.it>*. Well-run and conveniently located. The eclectic décor in this converted pasta factory may be stuck in another decade, but the helpful staff and harbour location, a stroll from the main square, make this a good option. Smallish contemporary rooms, most with balconies. 62 rooms.

Luna Convento €€€ *Via Pantaleone Comite 33, 84011, tel: 089-871002, fax: 089-871333, <www.lunahotel.it>*. Rebuilt in 1975, this former 13th-century convent still retains gorgeous Romanesque cloisters, a baroque chapel, and a 15th-century Saracen tower that now houses one of the Luna's two restaurants and bars. Close by are the hotel's private rocky beach and seaside saltwater pool. 40 rooms.

Santa Caterina €€€€ *Strada Amalfitana 9, 84011, tel: 089-871012, fax: 089-871351,<www.hotelsantacaterina.it>*. Owned by the same family for generations, another of the coast's venerable hotels, carved into multiple levels of a cliff, an easy walk from town. Old-world and comfortably elegant, the hotel has a saltwater pool, lush terraced gardens, glorious views, a small private beach and respected restaurant – all further enhanced by a warm, friendly, helpful staff. 66 rooms and suites.

Recommended Restaurants

Neapolitan home cooking is Italian cuisine at its best. Always look for the unpretentious trattorias where you're sure to find the regional specialities in a characteristic family-run ambience. But even a deceptively simple dinner of fresh seafood can mean high prices: you can easily move into a higher price range with a first-course of pasta and a main course of grilled fish from local waters. Order with care and there won't be any surprises. Off-season closures (from a few weeks to a few months) can change from one year to the next depending upon that year's high-season business. Always call in advance, especially in the 'shoulder season', to make sure the establishment is still open. When possible, book in advance during the busy high season months. All the following take credit cards except where noted. The following price categories are merely an indication of the average meal for one, consisting of three courses with a house wine.

€€€   50 euros and up
€€   25–50 euros
€   25 euros or below

NAPLES

Amici Miei €€ *Via Monte di Dio 78, Chiaia, tel: 081-764 6063.* Small, dark and intimate restaurant, long loved for its meat specialities and classic pastas. This being Naples, fresh seafood is given its fair share of attentive preparation: no one leaves disappointed, especially after sampling the homemade fruit tarts. Lunch and dinner Tuesday–Saturday, Sunday lunch only.

Brandi € *Salita S. Anna di Palazzo (corner of Via Chiaia), tel: 081-416928, <www.brandi.it>.* Never mind that the pizza Margherita (the classic version with mozzarella and tomato sauce named after King Umberto's queen) is said to have been born here in 1889. This is Naples' oldest *pizzeria* (with a full *trattoria* menu), and still one of its most frequented, by celebs (signed photos plastered everywhere), locals and tourists alike. Cosy and bustling indoors, with a few tables outside on a narrow alleyway. No credit cards. Lunch and dinner daily.

Caffè Gambrinus € *Piazza Trieste e Trento, tel: 081-417582, <www.caffegambrinus.com>.* The city's most famous and theatrical *caffè*, this 19th-century landmark near the Palazzo Reale is still a stylish watering hole for all strata of local society and intelligentsia, as well as savvy visitors who enjoy the people-watching. Light meals, famous pastries and ice creams, or just a coffee or cappuccino secure a table at the grandly vaulted indoor salons or outdoors. A pianist or Viennese orchestra add to the experience. Open daily, 8–2am.

Ciro a Santa Brigida €€ *Via Santa Brigida 71, tel: 081-552 4072, <www.ciroasantabrigida.com>.* Since opening in 1932, this has been an institution for regulars including Toscanini and Pirandello. Off the store-lined Via Toledo, the two-storey restaurant is always busy. Pizzas or a lengthy menu of classic Neapolitan dishes served by *simpatico* house-proud waiters. Lunch and dinner, Monday–Saturday.

Da Michele € *Via Sersale 1, tel: 081-553 9204.* Brandi may have the history and glamour, but those in the know reckon that this humble establishment in the historic centre serves the finest pizza in Naples (and thus the world). Prepare to queue and choose either margerita or marinara (nothing else is on offer). No credit cards.

La Cantinella €€–€€€ *Via N. Sauro 23, Lungomare, tel: 081-764 8684, <www.lacantinella.it>.* Fresh seafood and classic Neapolitan specialities at their finest. In a sophisticated atmosphere of relaxed luxury, splurge on the best from the fish market's daily offerings, with imaginative dishes for the less traditional. Meat lovers won't be disappointed; impressive wine list. Lunch and dinner, Monday–Saturday.

La Sacrestia €€€ *Via Orazio 116, tel: 081-761 1051, <www. lasacrestia.it>.* Impeccable service, superb seafood, and a hilltop terrace setting for a twinkling dinner-with-view make this one of Naples' most famous restaurants. Located above the Mergellina area and long known for its serious preparation of Neapolitan classics, a new generation has infused some more contemporary interpretations into this 'temple of Neapolitan gastronomy.' Lunch and dinner; closed Sunday dinner and Monday lunch.

La Scialuppa €€ *Borgo Marinari 5, tel: 081-764 5333*. One of the most charming of the many traditional seafood restaurants in the fisherman's quarter at the foot of Castel dell'Ovo. Sit beside the water listening to the buskers, watching the yachts and eating luscious fresh pasta with seafood and scarlet cherry tomatoes. Closed Monday.

Scaturchio € *Piazza San Domenico Maggiore 19, tel: 081-551 6944*. A wonderfully atmospheric stand-up affair that is the quintessential Neapolitan *bar/pasticceria*, this venerable century-old landmark showcases the local art of pastry-making at its best. Policemen, nuns, hipsters and grandmothers come here for excellent coffee and local specialities such as *babà al rhum*, *sfogliatelle* stuffed with sweetened ricotta cheese, and *ministeriale*, a chocolate cake with whipped rum-cream filling. Open 8am–10pm Wednesday–Monday. No credit cards.

Vini e Cucina € *Corso Vittorio Emanuele 762, tel: 081-660302*. There are just over a dozen tables and the price is right for local home-style cooking at its unpretentious best. So come on the early side if the Mergellina train station neighbourhood doesn't deter you, and be prepared to wait. The understandably popular simple spaghetti in a full-flavored *ragu* sauce is served as it was meant to be. Closed Sunday. No credit cards.

CAPRI

Ai Faraglioni €€€ *Via Camerelle 75, Capri Town, tel: 081-837 0320*. Fairly central (on the main strip) and well frequented by multinational patrons, this stylish restaurant has long been known as a place to see and be seen (particularly at its outdoor tables) and menu that leans towards nouvelle European, made with the finest of local ingredients. Open daily for lunch and dinner mid-March–October.

Aurora €€–€€€ *Via Fuorlovado 18–20, Capri Town, tel: 081-837 0181, <www.auroracapri.com>*. The Neapolitan tradition of pizza as an art form lives on here. A simple pizza and a home-made dessert make for a memorable meal, as confirmed by all the celebs whose autographed glossies grace the walls of this old-time favourite. Also offers full restaurant menu and extensive wine list. Daily, lunch and dinner; open March to December.

Da Gelsomina €€ *Via Migliara 72, Anacapri, tel: 081-837 1499, <www.dagelsomina.com>*. Part of a six-room *pensione* hideaway, this charming countryside spot with sweeping views is best for a leisurely lunch. Its *ravioli alla caprese* and homemade wine from its surrounding vineyard are two of many reasons to come here. Closed February. Open daily for lunch and dinner mid-June to mid-September; otherwise, generally lunch only.

Da Gemma €€ *Via Madre Serafina 6, Capri Town, tel: 081-837 0461*. Its relative proximity to the central Piazzetta and years of patronage by locals in the know have long secured this moderately priced favourite a certain renown. Authentic island specialities are served in a cosy 14th-century palazzo in winter, and on a lovely covered terrace in warm weather. The signature *fritta alla Gemma* is a medley of lightly fried fish, vegetables and mozzarella. Open daily, lunch and dinner; check for winter closing.

La Capannina €€ *Via Le Botteghe 12–14, Capri Town, tel: 081-837 0732, <www.capannina-capri.com>*. Located a brief stroll from the town's principal Piazzetta, this well-loved spot for local specialities attracts celebrity guests who enjoy good, unpretentious dining in the pergola-covered courtyard. The house wine, from the owner's island vineyard, pairs deliciously with home-made pasta and fresh fish. Open daily for lunch and dinner, mid-March to mid-January. Closed Wednesday off-season.

La Fontelina €–€€ *I Faraglioni (at the end of Via Tragara), Capri Town, tel: 081-837 0845*. Overlooking the dramatic offshore Faraglioni, this idyllic seaside spot serves lunch only on breezy bamboo-shaded terraces, with its own patch of rocky beach below. Fresh and refreshing, the fruit-filled white wine sangria sets the tone for a simple and simply delicious menu of homemade pasta and the best of the local fish market's morning delivery. Its competitor, Da Luigi, is just next door, with an equally impressive setting and slightly more expensive menu. Open daily for lunch only, April to mid-October.

Caruso €€ *Via Sant'Antonino 12 (Piazza Tasso), tel: 081-807 3156, <www.ristorantemuseocaruso.com>.* This much favoured old-timer is an homage to both the revered Neapolitan tenor (who spent a lot of leisure time in Sorrento) and to local Campanian specialities. Both evoke the romance of old Naples, further enhanced by the fading posters, opera memorabilia and original recordings of the tenor that are usually played in this slightly kitsch, characterful setting. Lunch and dinner daily; closed Mondays off-season.

Don Alfonso 1890 €€€ *Piazza Sant'Agata, Sant'Agata sui Due Golfi, tel: 081-878 0026, fax: 081-533 0226, <www.donalfonso.com>.* Pilgrims of gastronomy know the 7-km (4.5-mile) drive from Sorrento to the hills 365m (1,200ft) above sea level is a price willingly paid for a meal at one of Italy's finest and most renowned restaurants, the proud holder of two Michelin stars. The exquisite ingredients used in the inventive, regionally-influenced cuisine come largely from the owners' farm. The award-winning wine cellar is one of the largest and best in Italy (and that's saying something). Elegant and expensive, serious food and wine lovers will love this experience and the warmth of the gracious Iaccarino family, who have run a restaurant here for over 100 years. There are rooms if you wish to stay. Open mid-April to October, lunch and dinner. Closed Monday and Tuesday (open Tuesday evening June to September). Advance booking essential.

O'Parrucchiano €€ *Corso Italia 67, tel: 081-878 1321, <www.parrucchiano.com>.* A large family-run establishment on the town's main drag that is always full of tourists, this famous eatery may first appear as a tourist trap. And it is. But it is reliable, foreigner-friendly, and a reasonably-priced locale, understandably nicknamed 'La Favorita'. Classic Sorrentine specialities (especially the first-course pastas and daily-changing fresh fish offerings) are well-prepared in a lovely conservatory redolent of the restaurant's early days in the 1890s. Lunch and dinner daily; closed Wednesday off-season.

POSITANO

Buca di Bacco €€ *Via Rampa Teglia 8, tel: 089-875699, <www.bucadibacco.it/restaurant.htm>*. Together with Chez Black, one of the most enduring of the beachfront see-and-be-seen scenes, a second-storey arbor-covered restaurant (book early for the railing-side tables with a view of the action below) has been making great strides in recent years to recoup some of its fading reputation. Its best main courses are the simply-grilled fresh fish. A pre-dinner drink at the first-floor open-sided bar is *de rigueur*. Open daily for lunch and dinner. Closed November to mid-March.

Chez Black €–€€€ *Via del Brigantino 19, tel: 089-875036, <www.chezblack.it>*. A stylish 'in' restaurant, one of a cluster snuggled directly on the beach, that offers very good quality and value-for-money considering its prime location and long-time popularity. For an informal lunch or relaxed dinner, it's one of the better choices in town for great pizzas and pastas, with reliably fresh fish for more serious dining. Open daily, March to early January.

Da Adolfo € *Località Laurito, tel: 089-875022*. A seductive glimpse of *la dolce vita* endures effortlessly at this casual outdoor restaurant reached only by motorboat (from Positano's main pier every 30 minutes 10am–1pm). Come for a simple, superbly fresh meal of home-cooked pasta, grilled mozzarella wrapped in lemon leaves and grilled fish, then hire a lounge chair or umbrella for a few idyllic beach hours. Lunch served daily; open May to mid-October. No credit cards.

Donna Rosa €€ *Via Montepertuso 97, Montepertuso, tel: 089-811806*. Worth every euro of the taxi ride up to this one-road town in the hills above Positano, this small, surprisingly refined restaurant is a very special family-run operation that leaves most of Positano's restaurants in the dust. Lunch is slow and relaxed, but dinner is always packed: word has travelled fast that this is a deliciously special dining option worth the 15-minute journey. A trio-sampling of homemade pastas followed by anything from the sea's bounty is a guaranteed experience. Closed early November to early December. Dinner daily; check for months when lunch is also offered.

RAVELLO

Cumpà Cosimo €–€€ *Via Roma 44, tel: 089-857156.* The best and best known in town for good home cooking and *trattoria* ambience. Regional dishes served in generous proportions with many ingredients from the family farm. A series of seven different sample-size pastas, each more delicious than the last, leaves little room for the mixed grill of fish, or any of the meat specialities from the owner's butcher's shop next-door. Open daily for lunch and dinner; closed Monday off-season. Closed mid-January to mid-March.

Villa Maria €€ *Via Santa Chiara 2, tel: 089-857255, <www.villa maria.it>.* Relaxed yet refined, this is one of the prettiest settings for lunch with a bird's-eye panorama, or for dinner with a high romance quotient. Classical music drifts through the pergola-covered alfresco terrace and cosy indoor dining room of this century-old villa that also offers a dozen rooms. The chef knows his regional specialities, beginning with the home-made spaghetti-like *scialatielli*. Open daily for lunch and dinner; winter closures vary.

AMALFI

Da Gemma €€ *Via Fra Gerardo Sasso 9, tel: 089-871345.* For more than 100 years one of the town's favourites, this family-owned restaurant sits a short walk from the cathedral with a second-storey open terrace that overlooks the main street. Pastas are prepared with tomato-based sauces made with seafood, and a thick *zuppa di pesce* (fish soup) is one of the recommended main-course specialities. Open daily for lunch and dinner. Closed mid-January to mid-February; closed Wednesday off-season.

La Caravella €€€ *Via Matteo Camera 12, tel: 089-871029, <www. ristorantelacaravella.it>.* A throwback to when the *dolce vita* jet-set put Amalfi on the vacation circuit. The art deco décor is the setting for what is still considered one of the area's most serious restaurants. A tasting menu familiarises guests with the coastline's specialities as interpreted by a nouvelle cuisine-inspired kitchen. Lunch and dinner daily; closed Tuesday off season. Closed November.

INDEX

Berlitz pocket guide

Naples, Capri & the Amalfi Coast

Tenth Edition 2008

Written by Patricia Schultz
Revised by Cathy Muscat
Updated by Melissa Shales
Edited by Jeffery Pike
Series Editor: Tony Halliday

Photography credits
4 Corners 99; Alamy 18; Bridgeman Art
Library 17; Chris Coe 8, 13, 15, 20, 22, 26, 29,
34, 37, 38, 40, 42, 43, 45, 50, 53, 54, 60, 63, 65,
68, 77, 78, 82, 84, 102; Hemis 96; Cathy Muscat
58; Tony Perrottet 2; Photoshot 68, 94; Bill
Wassman 87; Phil Wood 1, 6, 11, 24, 31, 32, 46,
47, 49, 54, 57, 66, 71, 72, 73, 74, 100

Cover picture: Demetrio Carrasco/Jon
Arnold Images

Printed in Singapore by Insight Print
Services (Pte) Ltd, 38 Joo Koon Road,
Singapore 628990. Tel: (65) 6865-1600.
Fax: (65) 6861-6438

Berlitz Trademark Reg. U.S. Patent Office
and other countries. Marca Registrada

Every effort has been made to provide
accurate information in this publication,
but changes are inevitable. The publisher
cannot be responsible for any resulting
loss, inconvenience or injury.

Contact us

At Berlitz we strive to keep our guides as
accurate and up to date as possible, but if you
find anything that has changed, or if you have
any suggestions on ways to improve this guide,
then we would be delighted to hear from you.

Berlitz Publishing, PO Box 7910,
London SE1 1WE, England.
fax: (44) 20 7403 0290
email: berlitz@apaguide.co.uk
www.berlitzpublishing.com